BUTLER AREA PUBLIC LIBRARY

BUTLER, PA.

PRESENTED IN MEMORY OF

Alice Foust

by

Marlene Musick

P9-AQU-456

198

SHOWCASE OF INTERIOR DESIGN

Eastern

747
SHO

Third Edition

BUTLER PUBLIC LIBRARY
BUTLER, PENNSYLVANIA 16001
169 5597

ROCKPORT PUBLISHERS
GLOUCESTER, MASSACHUSETTS
DISTRIBUTED BY NORTH LIGHT BOOKS
CINCINNATI, OHIO

Copyright © 1997 by
Rockport Publishers, Inc.

All rights reserved. No part of this book may be
reproduced in any form without written permission
of the copyright owners. All images in this book
have been reproduced with the knowledge and prior
consent of the artists concerned and no responsibility
is accepted by producer, publisher, or printer for
any infringement of copyright or otherwise, arising
from the contents of this publication. Every effort
has been made to ensure that credits accurately
comply with information supplied.

First published in the United States of America by:
Rockport Publishers, Inc.
33 Commercial Street
Gloucester, Massachusetts 01930-5089
Telephone: (508) 282-9590
Facsimile: (508) 283-2742

Distributed to the book trade and art
trade in the United States by:
North Light Books, an imprint of
F & W Publications
1507 Dana Avenue
Cincinnati, Ohio 45207
Telephone: (800) 289-0963

Other Distribution by:
Rockport Publishers, Inc.
Gloucester, Massachusetts 01930-5089

ISBN 1-56496-415-9

10 9 8 7 6 5 4 3 2 1

Book Design by:
Sara Day Graphic Design

Manufactured in China

TABLE OF CONTENTS

PROLOGUE

Manhattan is headquarters for more interior designers than any other piece of real estate in the world. The profession of interior design got its start on this sophisticated and densely populated island. As the ripples of better design move out across North America and around the world, the Eastern region consistently produces leaders of the evolving professional field. New York, Boston, Philadelphia, Washington, and other Eastern centers have become headwaters for much that is most admired in refined home fashions. We are therefore particularly interested in the designers whose work has been selected for this edition of *Showcase of Interior Design*.

Our mission continues to be education. *Showcase of Interior Design* presents the best work of the most talented designers: young and old, modernists and traditionalists, and every combination between. Our editors search for an eclectic range of style and levels of cost. Good design is not necessarily elaborate or lavishly expensive. We are not arbiters of faddish trends or self-appointed taste-setters; our purpose is to empower our readers with information that will allow them to manage the design process. We hope our readers will learn how to select an interior designer that is a good fit for their tastes and budgets.

As one very famous member of the New York design profession said to me, "Nobody ever died of a bad decorating job." In that spirit, please relax and enjoy the process of creating a welcoming, comforting home. Another bit of design advice to remember: "It's a living room, not a dead room."

—John Aves

Design firm:

Jean Valente

Getting Comfortable with Your Designer

To live better and derive the most pleasure possible from your surroundings, it is important that your home be in sync with your spirit, the very personal core of uniqueness that defines who you are.

Using a trial-and-error approach to decorate your home, hoping to come up with that ideal combination—comfortable enough for living but impressive enough for guests—usually doesn't result in that special quality you seek. A professional interior designer is just what the name implies—a professional—trained and practiced in bringing beauty to interiors.

Whether you're furnishing a one-bedroom apartment or an elaborate country- or town-house, a designer will give it that special panache. Perhaps you want everything new or an update to reflect changed tastes. A true professional can create an environment that is user-friendly, dazzling, and in perfect accord with the way you want to live.

The furniture marketplace offers choices so vast that it is often overwhelming and your space may be a puzzle. These are the challenges designers deal with all the time. Their expertise solves these problems, and makes it a pleasurable experience for you. They reduce anxiety and give you confidence by establishing an overall plan.

An interior designer can help

you make choices in furniture.

Design firm: Francis-Russell

Specifically, designers do the following:

- Clarify your design and focus on a style that speaks to your heart. Whether it's traditional, contemporary, country or formal, designers will, together with you, develop a plan
- With fabric, paint and floor covering, they create a color palette that is richly satisfying
- Size up your space and draft a floor plan for furniture arrangement that meets your needs and includes good traffic patterns
- Devise a budget plan and time schedule of furniture purchases that is comfortable for you
- Pull together art and accessories for a polished look

Your designer will be your partner as choices and decisions have to be made. He or she will be your guide to planning a home of good taste to stand the test of time. Interior designers are practiced hunters and gatherers. They show you fabrics, rugs and furniture that non-professionals would be hard-pressed to locate. With expertise, he can instruct painters who glaze your walls and decorative artists who fashion designs on your floors. Well-decorated rooms are full of nuances that really only come off when planned by an expert.

How To Find The Right Interior Designer

Getting the right designer requires a little ESP and a close analytical look. To arrive at that very personal haven you deserve, you must work with someone with whom you truly communicate and enjoy a natural rapport. Mutual trust is important. You'll be spending a lot of time together, so choose someone who's comfortable to be around.

There are several ways to find a good designer. Looking through *Showcase of Interior Design* is a start. Read it with an eye to what is pleasing to you. Keep a scrapbook of rooms you like in shelter magazines and note who did them. In addition, ask people whose taste and style you respect for referrals. High-quality retail stores can be a fine source, as are the design centers of most major cities. Visit showhouses and keep a list of whose work appeals to you. If you consult the Yellow Pages, look for members of professional organizations like the American Society of Interior Designers (ASID).

Interview several with an eye to their design style and personality. When reviewing portfolios, remember you are seeing input from a designer's clients as well as their own work. Determine if the designer will listen and take into consideration the possessions you already have. You want someone who will respect your collections, travel mementos, and your sentimental pictures, and who will display them in a manner both interesting and appropriate.

An interior designer combines your possessions with

new furnishings to create a comfortable setting.

Design firm: Solis-Betancourt

Get client references—ask them how the designer solved their problems. If something arrived in the wrong color or fabric, did the designer go to bat for the client? What about work habits? Was the designer on time and available when needed? Most important, trust your instincts.

How To Work With An Interior Designer

A good designer will ask a lot of questions about how you live. Be candid and say what you think. It is as important to mention what you don't like as it is to show what you do. The better you and the designer know and understand each other, the better the result. In a sense, designers have to be analysts. They must ask a lot of leading questions in order to create your "machine for living."

A designer needs to know how you use your space—so be aware of your living habits. Make lists, no matter how unimportant you think something is. Don't assume a decorator can read your mind. If, for example, you have a lot of shoes and need special storage, mention it early.

Understanding your design needs at the beginning of a job ensures your designer's creative energy is spent efficiently and time is not wasted. Tell him or her as much as you can about your lifestyle. A good designer will ask key questions, for example, "Where do you enjoy watching television?" "Do you work at home?" "How frequently do you entertain?" "How many people do you need to seat at your dining table?" "How much storage do you need?"

You—your personality and taste—are the most important factors your designer has to work with. Your rooms should reflect you as perfectly as do your clothes. If you share your home with family or others, be sure to include their opinions. Do your homework together. Visit furniture shops, accessory boutiques and antique shops (if your taste includes a love of old things). Ask yourself and each other which items you'd buy and which accents you would choose to complement them.

To spark your designer's creative talents, show him or her examples of possessions you love. A rug, mirror, or painting that speaks to you can be a helpful guide in putting together a home that says "you." Keep your mind open to the suggestions of your professional decorator. Just because your television or armoire has always been on one wall doesn't mean it can't be moved. Don't let your own preconceptions put limits on your design plan.

With your decorator, inventory all your furniture. Decide what pieces you'll keep, what you'll keep temporarily and what you'll eliminate. Be clear about these intentions. Your designer can change and enhance many items by painting, recovering or reupholstering. A broken family heirloom can be given new life.

Being a strong-minded client with your own opinions is not the nemesis to a designer that you may imagine it could be. When your opinions reflect an important truth, they actually help. Best results are achieved when you have a lot of input and there is a continuous back-and-forth between you and your designer.

Keep an open mind to a designer's ideas, and he or she will

be empowered to design rooms spectacular as this one.

Design firm: Nancy Mullan Interiors, Inc.

Make a dream list of what you'd include in your home if given carte blanche—and unlimited financial resources. Don't limit yourself; if you've always wanted a home theater or gym, jot it down. Only when designers know your dreams can the designer make them happen. When you really don't know what you want, a designer can teach you what changes can improve your life. Then, when you go shopping in the company of your designer, visiting large design centers and to-the-trade-only showrooms, you'll be able to focus on what you need.

How To Set Up Your Budget

Professional design assistance protects your investment in your home. Acquiring furnishings is a continuing and substantial investment. Have an idea of furniture prices and hourly rates for labor so you can set a realistic figure. Be clear about your budget. Remember, if what you

Purchase the highest quality pieces your budget will allow—it will be less expensive in the long run.

Design firm: Tonin MacCallum, ASID Inc.

favor includes French antiques and opulent fabrics, you'll have to budget accordingly. A designer will work with you to establish an overall plan and prioritize purchases.

When you begin pricing furniture, you'll realize why a workable budget is so important. For major pieces, getting the best you can afford pays off because you won't have to replace those items so quickly. Collaborate closely with your decorator to determine how and where moneys are spent. For example, if you have a job in which you are likely to be transferred every few years, your decorator can help you plan to invest the major part of your allotment on quality pieces that can travel with you and work in many settings. Good budgeting also prevents impulse-buying and spending too much on a minor item. Most important, designers save you money by preventing you from making costly mistakes.

How Interior Designers Charge For Their Services

Designers vary in their methods of billing. Some charge an overall design fee. Others work on an hourly rate based on experience and reputation or they add on a percentage to the purchases you make. Some use a combination of these methods. You may be billed for consultation and floor plan. It's possible, depending on the scope of the project, to arrange a flat fee.

A "percentage over net" means the designer gets furnishings at a trade discount or wholesale price, passing on that savings to you. His design fee or percentage is his compensation. The net price plus the designer's fee approximates retail.

Be sure to have your designer put your financial agreement in writing.

No matter what your budget,
a designer will make it work.
Design firm: Jean P. Simmers, Ltd.

How To Create A Design Team

When should your interior designer come to the job? Ideally, a designer should be hired the day you hire your architect and contractor because of the practical benefits his broad fund of knowledge and experience bring. Their working together gives you a better project. Here are eight benefits:

- A savvy designer can integrate the furniture plan with the architect's design
- Your designer can specify lighting fixtures, color and placement of outlets, special materials, new products
- Your designer can work with the contractor to keep up the momentum
- Your designer can supervise telephone and stereo setups, insuring correct positioning
- A designer is skilled at reading an architect's or contractor's drawings and will know when hallways are too tight, or when walls are incorrectly or unwisely placed to accommodate your furniture
- Your designer's awareness of design, products, and aesthetically pleasing ways of doing things can be part of the initial building project instead of add-on costs later
- Together with your contractor, a designer can help create a comprehensive "punch list" of details that must be completed correctly before your contractor receives final payment

A designer can work with the architect and contractor to communicate your wishes.
Design firm: Joanne DePalma Inc.

A designer can help keep your space from
becoming a casualty of the Information Age.
Design firm: T. Keller Donovan, Inc.

When a designer understands the entire scope of the job, he can schedule decorative artists, furniture deliveries, window treatments, and lighting accordingly so the construction and the furnishings are completed at the same time

Why Today's Homes Need Professional Designers

With the impact of electronics on the home, home theaters, home offices, home spas and the re-prioritizing of space to accommodate our 21st-century lifestyle, the traditional home is being reconfigured. Today's designer is aware of how to incorporate the latest technical advances and still maintain wonderful colors, fabrics, trims, and fine art for a home that is beautifully detailed and eminently comfortable. Interior design is an art form. Your home is your masterpiece. Choose a muse that will give voice to your innermost dreams. Savor the process, then enjoy the adventure of mixing the paints and making the brushstrokes that create a grand design that will satisfy your soul.

—*Teri Seidman*

Antine
Associates

Anthony Antine
212.988.4096
201.224.0315

Antine Associates rooms are designed to be grand and elegant, but more importantly, for comfort and function. The firm feels there is no reason why you cannot achieve both.

Reading or relaxing by the fire on a "tête-à-tête" designed by Antine—formality with a huge accent on comfort.

The upholstered walls of the room add an extra warmth to this niche, which contains a drop arm sofa and a chinoise coffee table set with antique decanters and glasses.

The warmth of the room is achieved by using a mixture of elegant fabrics, fine antiques and collectibles, and wonderfully comfortable upholstery. The chinoise secretary is seventeenth century, the bull's eye mirror eighteenth century, and the rug late nineteenth century. The walls are upholstered in Scottish wool woven in a Russian pattern.

Antony Childs, Inc.

Kelly P. Flocks and
David H. Knight
1668 Wisconsin Avenue, NW
Washington
DC 20007
202.337.1100

Our firm provides clients with the utmost in quality, service, and discretion. By foregoing fads and trends and by using antique furniture, contemporary upholstery, and the finest fabrics and furnishings, we create comfortable, timeless interiors for our clients to enjoy for years to come.

This library, though elegant and sophisticated, appears inviting through the use of a neutral color scheme and soft, contemporary upholstery.

The Beaux Arts architecture of
the room, originally intended as
a dining room, was of a scale
not compatible with today's
lifestyles. The monumental size
of the room is camouflaged by
dividing the space into separate
seating and dining areas.

A collection of antique
leather books is partly
concealed behind simple
silk curtain panels.

David
Barrett,
Inc.

David Barrett
305 East 63rd Street
New York
NY 10021
212.688.0950

Approaching a project involves adapting a client's lifestyle and needs to his or her space through design and decoration. Where a space requires modification, the solution is based on enhancing the space for the client's needs. The final selections are based on an interpretation of the client's requirements into a harmonious composition of style and comfort.

Mirror and trompe l'oeil finishing in this dining room camouflage bad structural features and enhance the illusion of a ruin. A coral stone table appears to have fallen from the mural. The chandelier hangs from a painted rafter, while the sideboard against the mirror is a balcony balustrade.

In the manner of an eighteenth-century garden "folie," the bedroom gives the impression of a ruin within an old garden. The bed frame, night tables, and columns are painted in trompe l'oeil stone, adding to the mural's illusion of depth. The columns and night tables provide concealed storage.

In a his-and-hers master bath, the styling is that of a romantic Edwardian bath/dressing room. All millwork is mahogany with gilding. The sink vanities are designed as Chippendale bowfront chests. The drawers are doors for under-cabinet storage. An English mirror disguises the medicine cabinet.

H. R.
Beckman
Design

H. R. Beckman
3600 Conshohocken Avenue
Philadelphia
PA 19131
215.473.2106

As a widely traveled student of art and architecture, I add inconspicuous technology to yesterday and subtle elegance to tomorrow. Finding space where none seems to exist, I provide drama without ostentation.

A boring living room alcove, previously used only for storage and a desk, now provides beauty, storage, and dining with a granite-topped buffet, bronze-tinted mirror, dramatic lighting, and a stunning blue-based table that expands to seat ten.

The "boy-proof" upholstery is Naugahyde; thin grooved carpeting covers the walls to form a continuous bulletin board. Utilizing the offset space from a recessed trundle bed, an illuminated surround provides space for a phone and clock radio.

A "what might have been" restoration amidst turn-of-the-century grandeur in a reception hall: light taupe walls touched with gold, and a ceiling matched to the carved stone fireplace. Bronze sculpture and andirons, stone furniture, chirping birds, fish frolicking in a fountain, extensive plantings, and a telescope bring the glorious outdoors indoors.

Alexis E.
Benné
Interiors

Alexis Benné
100 Riverside Drive
New York
NY 10024
212.580.8118

The most exciting thing in life is to be challenged—that is what creativity is all about. All periods in history have given us a particular vision of beauty, and if you are addicted to beauty as I am and love what you do, then the joy of this profession is being able to work with different styles and personalities, creating homes that become my clients' private sanctuaries, surrounded by the things that personalize their home and make them smile. In that way, every home has its own soul.

Renovating a room not part of a historical house, the designer aimed for a contemporary nautical feeling more conducive to its summer residents. Previously dark, this room is now much lighter in feeling, with whisper white walls.

The dining room in this historical house, built circa 1750 and later relocated to an oceanfront site, possesses a wonderful Normandy feel. An oil portrait of Mrs. Baker—the original owner of the house—presides over the long room at last, after residing in the attic for some time. The color scheme is now brighter, bridging the past to the present.

This room was originally a music room. It no longer hears the sound of a piano, but it is a cheerful, engulfing room done in toile, colonial blue, and gingham, mixed with sunlight. A great room to daydream in.

William
Beson
Interior
Design

William Beson
275 Market Street,
IMS, Suite 530
Minneapolis
MN 55405
612.338.8187

Our designers interpret the client's practical and aesthetic needs to create the ideal environment. We pride ourselves on the versatility of our styles, which enables us to work with clients from a contemporary "less is more" attitude, to the lavish traditional interiors shown here. Our impeccable style is coupled with top-notch service and a sense of integrity that constantly drives us to strive for the very best.

The dining room of this turn-of-the-century home celebrates the art of fine dining. The mural, which envelopes the entire room, was influenced by nineteenth-century artist Albert Bierstadt and created by French mural artist Nicolas David.

This jewel box of a powder room, with its eclectic mix of elements, creates an intriguing and captivating space.

This trophy room with its amber color palette combines a number of varied finishes and textures to create a warm inviting ambience; a perfect place to enjoy a fine cognac and a great book.

Solis
Betancourt

Jose Solis Betancourt
1054 Potomac Street, NW
Washington
DC 20007
202.659.8734

Our ultimate goal is to individualize each project. We follow an academic approach to integrating architecture and interiors; at the same time, we strive to achieve function and comfort by means of proportion and harmony. Solis Betancourt has developed substantial experience with contemporary design through close working relationships with national and international consultants and contractors in lighting, textiles, antiques, contemporary furnishings, millwork, metallurgy, and conservation of all types. Through working with this select group, we assure efficient delivery of the design solution.

An antique Chinese textile becomes a unifying element in a serene master bedroom and commands the dreamy color palette.

Ancient Egyptian covered jars and animated Roman drinking vessels stand on guard and create an inviting processional in the entry halls of this art-filled residence.

Floor-to-ceiling reversible velvet panels add verticality and provide a seasonal change to this library. They also protect fine leather-bound books from harmful sunlight and dust.

Blair
Design
Associates,
Inc.

Debra A. Blair
315 West 78th Street
New York
NY 10024
212.595.0203

The relationship established between client and designer is the most important aspect of interior design. Good design doesn't just happen. Rather, it is a process that merges the uniqueness of the client with the designer's ability to interpret. More than a decade of experience has shown us that mutual commitment at the beginning makes for wonderful results in the end.

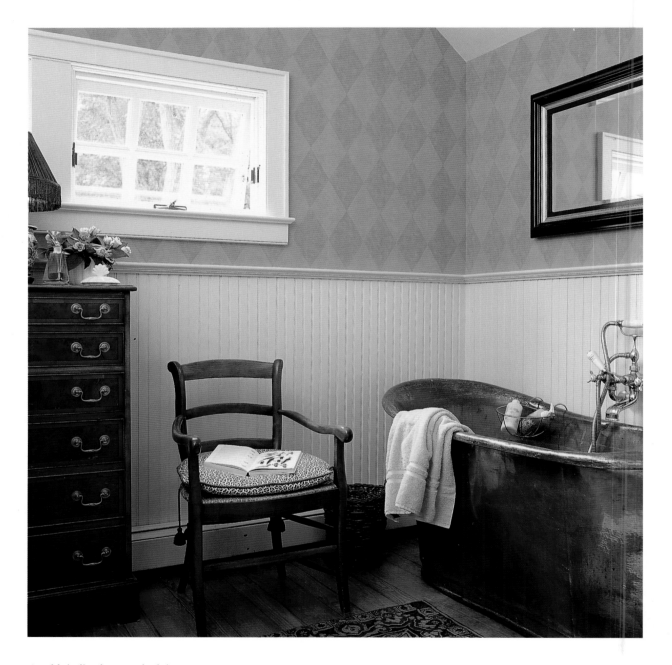

An old tin-lined copper bath is both a visual pleasure and surprisingly comfortable tub. The wall-mounted faucet with hand shower is a reproduction. Warm pink harlequin wallpaper above the wainscoting complements the rosy undertones of the cherry furniture.

Large ceramic tiles on the floor, stucco walls, and a rich ochre paint color work together to evoke a Tuscan Farm House style in this newly renovated kitchen in New Jersey.

A teak-lined ceiling and beams and faux limestone painted walls add architectural interest where there was none. Sisal carpeting installed wall to wall creates a textural background for the large-scale sofa and bed to inspire a look that is bold, tailored, and lush.

**L.B.D.A.
Design
Associates,
Inc.**

Laura Bohn
30 W. 26th Street, #11
New York
NY 10010
212.645.3636

Our aesthetic combines contemporary minimalism, antiques, custom designed furniture, and unexpected color palettes. We have designed residences, restaurants, and stores in New York, California, Japan, and Saudi Arabia, as well as motion picture sets and photo shoots. In addition to architectural and interior design projects, we have designed furniture, fabrics, and wall coverings that reflect a sensual exploration of textures. The work of Lembo Bohn Design has been featured in numerous publications, including *The New York Times, New York Magazine, Elle Decor, HG, Interior Design,* and *Martha Stewart Living.*

This romantic dining room features some of the firm's favorite colors and materials: chartreuse walls, gauze drapes, mohair upholstery, and rubbed wood.

A freestanding wall divides the bedroom from the dressing area by turning a closet into an architectural element.

A mix of antique chairs with Fortuny upholstery and modern architecture creates a contemporary and romantic setting in this restaurant.

Patricia
Bonis
Interiors

Patricia Bonis
8 Fairway Court
Cresskill
NJ 07626
201.894.9082

Good communication between the client and the designer is the cornerstone of a successful project. The client's personality and aesthetic desires must be properly interpreted by the designer in order to create a tasteful and appropriate result. Talent, experience, and inspiration perform no less vital a mission in enabling the designer to discern the timeless from the fleeting, thereby realizing the potential beauty and utility of every space.

A warm color scheme, mixed patterns, and beautiful wood moldings transform this large, open space into an intimate setting.

This kitchen design fulfills the client's love of French country style while satisfying the utilitarian requirements of a full working kitchen that accommodates a family of five.

In laying out this master bathroom, the designer kept in mind the eye-opening garden view.

Samuel
Botero
Associates,
Inc.

Samuel Botero
420 East 54th Street, Suite 34G
New York
NY 10022
212.935.5155

It is the interior designer's responsibility to assist clients in clarifying their vision and to apply his or her own knowledge and expertise towards the realization of the project. Interior design is a team effort. The designer represents the creative force that brings together all the talents that make up the final solution in an environment. A good plan that meets all of the functions required by the client represents the backbone of a successful project. The simple and direct design solution always feels comfortable and right to the eye.

This room is a combination library and dining room, as the clients frequently dine out when in New York and did not require a full dining room.

The clients of this New York City apartment wanted a feeling of permanence and comfort for this second residence. The apartment faces the East River and receives abundant light. Soft and romantic window treatments were planned to accommodate the intense morning sun and the apartment's heating units.

Brett
Design
Inc.

Brett Beldock
201 East 87th Street
New York
NY 10128
212.987.8270

The interior design process should be an enjoyable experience. Clients are asked to close their eyes and imagine—to visualize the space they would most like to live in and work in. There are really no "rights" or "wrongs" in decorating. It is a matter of creating spaces that function and fulfill clients' wishes. Rooms can often speak to you. You can borrow from their existing details, feel the color they should be, while you determine the room's use and function.

Each space should be a reflection of its owner. As the designer, I introduce ideas and richness to further add to a client's visualization, executing their wishes beyond their dreams.

Striè cashew colored walls and

hand-painted panels grace a living

room/salon.

This striè entry gallery with
red chinoiserie clock leads to
a red library.

Lacquer red library/guest room.

Sheila
Britz
Home

Sheila Britz, ASID
1196 Lexington Avenue
New York
NY 10028-9998
212.517.5153

Sheila Britz stresses refined style, durability, and a blending of color and fabrics wed to a wide range of budgets and styles. An independent designer who has spent more than fifteen years specializing in the design and renovation of residences in the greater New York area, she recently launched a retail design and furnishings store, Sheila Britz Home. Britz feels that the study of light and texture drew her to interior design from the beginning.

Green marble, mahogany, and brass finishes create the atmosphere of a formal English gentleman's dressing room and bathroom.

Meticulous attention to detail is evident in the window treatments, custom upholstery, fabrics, and decorative objects of this Upper East Side bedroom in New York City.

The designer used mahogany wood, leather-bound books, and paisley fabric in a Park Avenue library.

Mario
Buatta
Inc.

Mario Buatta
120 E. 80th Street
New York
NY 10021
212.988.6811

"Mario Buatta has maintained his enduring niche by polishing his own classic vision...rather than by second-guessing fashion. [His] refined but opulent interiors seem to have accumulated like an old family trust—from a genteel lifetime of measured collecting. 'As a designer, you're constantly absorbing,' Buatta explains. 'It's like being a writer. It's not that he or she is inspired every day, but the writer keeps absorbing ideas, characters, situations. You see things that you remember from the past connecting. It all comes together as a whole.' Not surprisingly, London loads him with ideas."—*Traditional Home Magazine*

The blue glazed walls in a criss-cross glazed finish reflect old blue jeans; the white and blue faux-tile floor pattern was taken from an old American quilt. A wicker trunk at the foot of the bed and the Chippendale faux bamboo chair counteract the weight of the other furnishings.

Green glazed walls and a pale sky blue ceiling decorate this paneled drawing room. Accents of geranium red and bottle green give this room a cozy and warm spring-like look throughout the year.

The opposite end of the drawing room features a second seating area. Windows are treated with festoon curtains of vibrant striped fabric. Two niches are filled with books set between eighteenth-century botanical design porcelain brackets.

45

CDM
Designs,
Inc.

Cathi Mankowski
20 Reservoir Road
Melville
NY 11747
516.549.0050

Beauty is subjective. In order to create a beautiful space, two philosophies are essential: First, always listen to your clients. The successful design of their home is a team effort. Second, be true to your materials. CDM Designs won't try to falsify or "faux" any material. Spaces should be designed for the use of specific materials or finishes. Whatever that material is, use it don't fake it. The result of the combination of those two philosophies is of course, a beautiful, quality, living environment.

A vaulted ceiling traveling the width of the space is complemented by a marquetry floor made of various woods. Blue marble tiles make an interesting mat. Antique elevator panels are the doors of the foyer closet.

A tray ceiling delineates the formal sitting area from the fireplace area and is framed by various moldings, rich in detail and glazed to add texture and depth. An expansion of glass from floor to ceiling allows an unobstructed view of the water.

English fiddleback sycamore cabinetry is complemented with gilded gold details that match the richness of the gold leaf crown ceiling.

Country
Design,
Inc.

Fiona Sigg, ASID
88 Elm Street
New Canaan
CT 06840
203.966.9131

As I approach a new job, certain considerations are paramount. If we are dealing with an empty house, I ask the clients to look through magazines and pick out their favorite rooms. Invariably this gives me an idea of which styles and colors they like. When clients already have existing pieces to begin with, we start from there. Then we discuss their lifestyle. Will they be doing a lot of entertaining? Are there small children and pets? These factors will be taken into consideration when we select fabrics and furnishings.

Raspberry faux finish and elegant woodwork create a striking dining room.

Warm yellow faux-finish walls accentuate a collection of English antiques.

A needlepoint rug and plaid taffeta drapes ground this panel study, and create a warm haven.

John M.
Davis
Interior
Design

John M. Davis
965 Fifth Avenue
New York
NY 10021
212.249.2891

As we approach the millennium, people want cleaner, lighter, less encumbered spaces. A good designer knows how to listen well to a client's needs and desires and to interpret those wishes in the best possible way, paying attention to practicality as well as appearance. It is most important nowadays that a designer be attuned to other aspects of life, particularly to the fashion world, the entertainment world, and the latest technology. A sense of humor and above all else—was the room completed last week, or twenty years ago?

Contemporary art juxtaposes an exquisite Louis XV bureau-plat and a Louis XV bergère in this Fifth Avenue home.

To accomplish an undecorated look, only one prominent pillow repeats the Hinson chintz used for the curtains on five windows in the living room of this large Bedford, New York home.

Symmetry is the substance of this Fifth Avenue dining room. The pair of doors lead into the living room. The Thomas Hope English Regency sideboard was found for the client in London. The aubergine lacquered walls were skim coated so many times that they act as a mirror to the rest of the room.

Mary W.
Delany
Interior
Design

Mary W. Delany
1 Strawberry Hill Court
Stamford
CT 06902
203.348.6839

The firm's designs respond to the client's needs and wishes, directly relating to the specific conditions and limitations of the building and its site. With an emphasis on comfort and pleasant surroundings, each project is custom designed with attention to the smallest detail. The client's budget and time schedule are always observed closely. The end result should beautifully express the client's desires, personality, and lifestyle.

A clerestory window was installed in this sunny, serene room to bring in more light but still keep the bed wall clear. The stained glass door, using the fabric as a theme, allows light from the master bath into the room.

The bay window was added to
provide space for the tub and to
bring light into the adjoining
master bedroom through a
stained glass connecting door.
A lovely pale color scheme
plays off the bedroom.

The room suits the beautiful
American Impressionist painting
of Giverny. A large room was
divided into seating areas
and other areas of interest.

Joanne
De Palma,
Inc.

Joanne De Palma
2109 Broadway, Suite 1570
New York
NY 10023
212.799.6088

Architecture inspires and guides me, along with the importance of interpreting my clients' desires and passions. Warmth and comfort, elegance without pretense, and most of all, restraint, is my challenge. I like to gently guide my clients into a place they didn't know they were going. As Diana Vreeland put it, "give them what they never knew they wanted." If we grow together, they make the discovery on their own and it's wonderful. That's part of the journey and the magic that makes it their home, not mine.

A bedroom writing area features stenciled and glazed walls, a Louis XVI writing table and painted eighteenth-century open armchairs.

Niche at the end of a hall holds a mahogany George III bonhur de deux jour, a white painted French box, and nineteenth-century Wedgewood creamware tweed bowl and vase.

A dining room on the Main Line in Philadelphia with monochromatic antique Chinese paper in the background supports an ever-growing and changing collection of English antiques and porcelain.

Michael
de Santis,
Inc.

Michael de Santis
1110 Second Avenue
at 58th Street
New York
NY 10022
212.753.8871

When approaching any design project, one must begin with establishing an understanding of the client's needs (function) as well as establishing an aesthetic rapport with the given space. Whether a room is contemporary or traditional, the key elements in a successful design scheme are balance and scale. The careful use of these two elements will add a timeless quality to an interior, appealing not only to the eye, but to all other senses.

An eighteenth-century carved gilt-wood console juxtaposed with artist Dennis Abbe's painted mural collectively form a dramatic presence and focal point of this drawing room. The soft palette of beiges and greys was adopted to define the scheme's understated elegance.

Rich jewel tones and opulent furnishings, such as the silk velvet upholstery and the nineteenth-century Aubusson rug, dominate this contemporary version of the Imperial style.

Shades of off-whites in variegated textures are combined with teak and cane furnishings to create a sophisticated Anglo-Indian mood in this tropical island retreat. Dominating the room is a British colonial-style four poster bed.

Diamond
Barratta
Design,
Inc.

William Diamond and
Anthony Baratta
270 Lafayette Street
New York, NY 10012
212.966.8892

We aim to create a fresh, colorful approach to design, whether it's an eighteenth-century American country house, a French chateau, or a Tribeca loft apartment. It all starts with great architecture and superior craftsmanship, both inside and out. We believe a home should suit one's personality and lifestyle. We design carpets, fabrics, and furniture specifically for our clients and combine them with beautiful antiques so their homes are unique and special.

Classic seaside charm in a breakfast room with blue and white sunflower fabric-covered walls and a black Portuguese needlepoint rug decorated with fruit and flowers.

A new kitchen and pantry was
designed with a colonial
revival feeling for a stately
Westchester home.

An elegant and comfortable master
bedroom suite for a home
designed in the eighteenth-century
French style. The room evokes a
Scandinavian influence.

D'Image Associates

Fran Murphy, ASID, CKD
71 E. Allendale Ave.
Saddle River
NJ 07458
201.934.5420

Every room I design must meet four criteria: First, it must delight the eye. Far beyond the initial impact of a beautiful room, it means small, carefully integrated touches, pleasing and charming to all. The second criterion is comfort. People respond to interiors that are warm and welcoming. Third, it must function appropriately. Families should be able to cook in their kitchens, to relax in their bedrooms, to work in their home offices, and be flexible in the ways they entertain. And, fourth, the decor should be timeless. The room must be able to withstand the changing whims of fashion.

Rubbed marble wall tiles with matching faux-painted hood, ceramic floor tiles masquerading as aged limestone, and hand-washed cabinets impart Old World charm to a thoroughly modern kitchen.

The owner's love of animals is reflected in a range of details, from elephants parading across the valance to the ceramic pieces that grace tabletops and bookshelves.

Barry Dixon, Inc.

Barry Dixon and Victoria Neale
2019 Q. Street, NW
Washington
DC 20009
202.332.7955

The integrity of good design is determined simply by what is "appropriate." To me, "appropriate" involves several levels of consideration. Architecture—what works well with the space—is paramount. Also important is transition, the thread that weaves through a home, simultaneously providing unity and flow and allowing diversion and interest. Comfort, even in the most formal areas, is mandatory, as is timelessness, straddling fad and period. Successful design emanates a feeling, not just a look. Nuance is employed to fine tune the whole to the personality of the individual.

Along the side of a formal room, a canted mirror casually reflects as much light and space as the flanking windows. A custom plaster ceiling is painted like the wall and trim for unity and height.

This end of a formal living
room opens onto a covered
loggia, allowing an unusual
blending of indoor and outdoor furnishings, including
a fire screen fashioned from
a garden gate. Mirrored surfaces add light and space.

A garden room is as formal as it
is informal. The key is freshness:
in color, pairing, and composition. An interesting corner was
created by repeating the window's silhouette in an upholstered screen.

T. Keller
Donovan
Inc.

T. Keller Donovan
30 East 60th Street
New York
NY 10022
212.759.4450

Good design speaks for itself. Achieving that end requires creativity, innovation, and resourcefulness, developing good client-designer relations, and having a roster of talented crafts people to execute our ideas. Each project is very important to us because our satisfied clients are our best publicity.

Despite an 8-foot (2.4-meter) high ceiling, visual height is achieved with shiny paint and curtains and bed panels hung from ceiling. One fabric is used extensively for an upholstered box effect.

Hunter green, which looks cool in summer and warm in winter, is used throughout this den, with white and black accents; the distinctive fabric was designed by the firm.

Cornices added to door frames and a smaller mantle give a better scale to a conventional room.

Gillian Drummond, Inc.

Gillian Drummond
55 Lewis Street, #5
Greenwich
CT 06830
203.629.3731

My desire is to create a timeless and uniquely personal environment in which my clients can enjoy their lives. A room should first serve its function, then be comfortable, luxurious, and inviting, but never take itself too seriously. The combination of color and texture with comfortable upholstery, beautiful wood, and distinctive art and accessories gives a room its personality and style. It should evolve and grow, as we do. However, the most important element in the creative process is the mutual trust and communication between the designer and client.

A collection of art and accessories found in the client's travels are effectively displayed in one part of the room.

The owners of this room inherited wonderful antique furniture, art, and accessories from family in Scotland. The challenge of making the rooms look up-to-date with color and fabrics that blend with the old upholstered pieces has given this room a fresh yet warm and timeless feeling.

The clients requested a room for their five-year-old daughter that will still be appropriate when she is fifteen. The color scheme keeps the room bright and pretty and the painted furniture gives it a romantic feeling that a young teenager will love.

Eberlein
Design
Consultants
Ltd.

Barbara Eberlein, ASID
1809 Walnut Street, Suite 410
Philadelphia
PA 19103
215.405.0400

Collaboration is the key to successful design, so we encourage an interactive process of mutual inspiration to arrive at personal expression. We search for what is unique in each client's aesthetic experience and set out to celebrate it in three dimensions. How are dreams transformed into reality? By maximizing the potential of every raw space through the careful analysis of each room's architectural merit, light quality, scale, proportion, balance, vistas and the rhythm of transition spaces...by creating a composition that, like a great novel or a great painting, achieves both dynamic excitement and subtle harmony.

This distinguished residence had most recently been used as a convent filled with altars, pews, and stained glass. Massive renovation efforts and interior architectural revisions made it suitable once again for residential use, and included re-defining the original parlor as the new living room.

The overwhelming dining room
was scaled to incorporate an
adjoining sitting room more suitable for a young active family. The
ethereal trompe l'oeil murals
throughout this elegant residence
were produced after researching
painted ceilings of Italian palazzi.

The sumptuous master suite
enjoys individual "his" and "hers"
bathrooms with adjacent dressing
rooms. "His" is a celebration of
fine craftsmanship in mahogany
and marble.

Francis-Russell
Design &
Decoration,
Inc.

Billy W. Francis / Ed Russell
NY: 212.980.4151
CA: 310.289.0332

Billy W. Francis and Associates, established in 1979 in Houston, attracted residential and commercial business from Houston's top stratum of social and business leaders. There Francis developed a mature style, characterized by gentle contemporary styling and a signature palette of textured neutrals richly accented with period furniture and other elements. He returned to New York at the height of the opulent 1980s market, when work was plentiful for the luxury interior design business.

This space provides an elevated area for entertaining, satisying a client's need for elegant dining and living.

The designers created an intimate seating area on a narrow stairwell landing of an elegant Beaux-Arts townhouse. High back sofa designed to shield owners from busy street noise.

Photo: Peter Vitale

This library—including state of the art video and audio equipment—showcases the owner's collection of antique toy cars and carriages.

Photo: Peter Vitale

Genauer-
Gold
Associates
Interior
Design

Ellen Genauer and Lenore Gold
515 East 72nd Street
New York
NY 10021
212.717.5847

The firm emphasizes interpreting the client's vision, tastes, and lifestyle into a beautiful and livable reality. Working closely and personally with the client, each design is a unique statement. Always respecting the architectural integrity of each residence—and seeking the best and most enduring examples of each period—the firm pays the utmost attention to scale, color, detail, and function.

The Louis XV-style desk with bronze ormolu mountings and gilt mirror above is a centerpiece in this gracious living room warmed by pale peach walls.

The hand-painted silk Chinese wallpaper, reproduced from an eighteenth-century design, is a subtle backdrop for this elegant drawing room. The French doors are a key architectural point of interest, and the painted paneling conceals an audio-visual center.

This traditional library, with its warm ambience, collection of fine eighteenth- and nineteenth-century paintings and furnishings, rich cherry woodwork, and savonnerie rug is a comfortable, functional, computer-equipped family room.

Yvette
Gervey
Interiors

Yvette Gervey
14 West 75th Street
New York
NY 10023
212.799.1740

Yvette Gervey creates beautiful and functional interiors that suit the individual tastes and personalities of her clients. She works carefully to balance and showcase light and shadow, and will search for the perfect furniture and accessories to match her clients' desired interiors.

In an area between the master bedroom and bath, once intended for closets, a meditation center provides a calming area. A mirrored wall reflects the light of authentic Japanese garden lanterns shaped like miniature pagodas.

In a house decorated in Japanese style, this muted and cozy den adjoins a light-filled living room, making the most of light and shadows. The unusual wall treatment is a textured simulation of bare, weathered greige concrete.

The master bath echoes the simple and elegant Japanese style used throughout the house, with teak floors, tub enclosure, and paneled walls. A Japanese bench and Oriental rug complete the look.

Marilyn Diane
Glass, Inc.
Interior
Design

Marilyn Diane Glass
311 East 38th Street
New York
NY 10016
212.286.8228

Essentially I am a classicist. For me a home should have a timeless quality, regardless of style. It should soothe, comfort, and reflect the clients' personal tastes and needs. My greatest challenge is to understand my clients' desires; to be sensitive to the things that are important to them. A love of simplicity and romance coupled with a strong sense of function is the essence of my work. A client once said to me, "You've changed my life; I can't wait to come home." My goal is to do that for every client.

Another approach to the classic style is this romantic music room designed to arouse the senses.

In this sleek living room of
classic furnishings from the
1920s and 1930s, a curved
Victorian chair evokes
another era.

In the same residence, timeless
English furnishings add warmth
and comfort to the modern
dining room.

Sue
Goldstein
Designs
Inc.

Sue Goldstein
The Studio at Rabbit Run
2445 River Road
New Hope
PA 18938
215.862.9898

A project must have a spine, and our goal is to create that spine and build the environment inside out. In-depth understanding of clients' taste, needs, and dreams is the foundation of my work. A broad range of resources are researched and collected to bring creativity and excitement to each new project. Good design does not just happen...It is a process of listening, collecting, integrating, and creating. A home is a backdrop of all that is important in life. Beautiful design does not have to be a dream.

A cedar truss system, put in for structural integrity as well as charm, replaced an old 8-foot (2.4-meter) ceiling in this garden room.

The antique Kelim rug sets the color scheme; the upholstery picks up the colors. The spirit of the room invites casual living.

This living room invites living and not just looking. A soft palette of color invites use with the help of textured fabrics and comfortable seating. All woodwork was painted to resemble pickled wood.

A casual mix of furnishings and a collection of antique Magolica pieces bring new life to this two-hundred-year-old Bucks County home. An antique baker's table serves as both a serving bar and as a space divider for two separate sitting areas.

Joan
Halperin/
Interior
Design

Joan Halperin
401 E. 80th Street
New York
NY 10021
212.288.8636

The design process is one of problem identification and solution. It starts with gathering information from my clients—listening to their needs and wishes—and then studying the space without preconception. I look to shape the space so that it is clean, cohesive, and clear, seamlessly integrating the functional and stylistic elements. Style and decoration can vary, but the basic plan and structure is key. At the decorating phase of the job, they are actively involved. The design process involves a partnership between client and designer—at its best, an exhilarating adventure.

Minimal furnishings create a

sophisticated pared-down look.

The monochromatic color scheme

of creamy whites, pale yellows, and

platinum is punctuated by dark

mahogany wood pieces.

The seamless continuity of this luxurious bathroom and dressing room, with its repeating curved elements, belie the fact that it was once three small rooms.

Pale Italian marble, warm mahogany cabinets, and a custom curved glass shower make this the favorite retreat of a suburban couple. A window seat with down pillows, in addition to a hidden phone and radio, invite them to linger.

Kenneth
Hockin
Interior
Decoration,
Inc.

Kenneth Hockin, ASID
Old Chelsea Station
Box 1117
New York
NY 10011
212.647.1955

Kenneth Hockin's interiors show respect for the time-honored traditions of period decoration, enlivened by a sophisticated palette and a predilection for comfort. He believes that successful designs result from updated interpretations of classic solutions and from dynamic collaborations between client and designer.

Venetian dining chairs, an English mahogany table, and an American Federal mirror complement each other beautifully in this grand dining room in Greenwich, Connecticut.

Designer Kenneth Hockin played mahogany antiques against the informality of mid-twentieth-century furnishings and fabrics in this casual seaside study in Southampton, Long Island.

Two separate sets of dining chairs are upholstered in the same linen damask and placed around a period George III mahogany table in the palatial dining room of a New York City townhouse.

Horne
International
Designs,
Inc.

C. Larry Horne, ASID
5272 River Road, Suite 450
Bethesda
MD 20816
301.656.4305

Designing for an international clientele, the various requirements of individuals or firms, appropriateness to architectural background, and creative use of space are primary concerns. Interpreting each project with the highest aesthetic discernment, the trademarks of my firm are suitability, quality, comfort, and creativity.

Elements of the British "Raj" in India accentuate this sun-filled garden room. A settee and chair of carved, painted teak provide seating around a faux leopard-skin floorcloth; a screen depicting European neo-classic architecture forms a backdrop amid a variety of plants.

An Eastern sitting room shows influences of Moroccan and Turkish ornaments and architecture.

An exercise and entertainment area for a home sports center boasts every possible amenity, from a full-sized billiard table to a private massage room.

HSP/Ltd.
Seglin
Associates

David A. Seglin
430 West Erie Street, Suite 510
Chicago
IL 60610
312.573.1300

Be inventive and flexible. Every project presents a new challenge. No site, building, client, or budget is ever the same. Exchange ideas—we contribute, the client contributes. Natural light, views, lifestyles, and precious objects are all important. Learning from one another, a direction is set, and problems can be solved. Make the client happy, make the project look good, make it so it will last. Modern? Classic? Traditional? Outrageous? As long as it's unique.

This 4000-square-foot (360-square-meter) city residence employs traditional detailing in a contemporary reinterpretation of a Victorian dwelling.

While encouraging a sense of horizontal connection, the plan articulates individual rooms and spatial sequences with columns and soffits. Shared space and framed views permit space to be visually "borrowed" from adjacent rooms.

A vacant department store that was being renovated into loft dwellings presented a unique palette of interior materials and finishes. The spiral stair leads to a rooftop penthouse, opening to the urban roof garden with an expansive view of the city.

Ingrao,
Inc.

Anthony Ingrao
150 E. 65th Street
New York
NY 10021
212.472.5400

Our studio's work is not defined by a particular "look"; the designer is both comforted by the beauty and craftsmanship of tradition, and inspired by the joy and color of contemporary life. We've always made the distinction between decoration and style: decoration makes the world a prettier place; style is memorable. Style is singular, growing from a particular person, place, and circumstance. Design for me is a playful process of discovering each client's personal style. It is an open-ended conversation between the sensibility and taste of the client and my intuitions and expertise.

Eighteenth-century paneling from France lines the walls of the main parlor. A unique design that incorporates structural beams at unusual angles brings symmetry to the room. Antique furnishings from Europe selected by the designer were placed in intimate settings.

A simple window treatment
that doesn't compete with the
magnificent view and antique
furnishings strikes a perfect
balance in this room.

The client was looking for a
children's playroom that wouldn't
look like a war zone when toys
were left out. The bright primary
colors allow toys to blend in and
become part of the design.

Interior Consultants

Denise Balassi
21 Fox Run
South Salem
NY 10590
914.533.2275

Over the past twenty years we have come to believe that successful design must be invisible. Great design does not call attention to itself: It is felt—never noticed. Each of our designs reflects the personality and lifestyle of our client. To achieve this, we serve as consultants and guides in the creative process. Consider us "ghost" designers. We turn unfathomable blueprints into homes and make tired old rooms exciting, welcoming, personal spaces.

Custom cabinetry and molding details help to create a traditional atmosphere that enhances the wonderful antique dining table and chairs. Traditional window treatments of silk are soft and striking. The overall effect is formal without being stuffy.

A canopy of lace adorns this four-poster bed in this very elegantly appointed bedroom. Archways were created here to delineate the sitting and dressing areas from the sleeping area of the very generously sized master bedroom suite.

Originally a basement, this cozy space now allows you to choose between watching a glowing fireplace, listening to music, watching television, or simply spending time relaxing with friends and family. The warm rich tones of wood envelope you into the space.

IDA
Interior
Design
Applications

Ida S. Goldstein, ASID
16 Munnings Drive
Sudbury
MA 01776
508.443.3433

Our design philosophy manifests itself in the rooms shown, where design style and client need intertwine: Taking full advantage of the sensational water view, the design suits the client's need for personal and business entertaining, yet serves as a comfortable home. Separating the long loggia into two areas is a freestanding custom cabinet of anigree wood accented with ebonized walnut. The informal side of the dining area sports a 70-inch television; the formal side creates the new dining space with an indoor garden.

The elegance of fine dining

in a garden setting.

This spectacular view is
enhanced by the play
of light and shadow.

A wonderful kitchen to

enjoy a delicious meal.

Interior Options

Ms. Michael Love
200 Lexington Ave., Suite 420
New York
NY 10016
212.545.0301

We want to have a reputation as a company where prospective clients feel comfortable turning to us to create the home they want to come home to, a company that listens to their concerns and acts on them in a positive manner; a company that is not deterred by the size and scope of the project; a company that understands that the little things really count; a company that gives them choices in how they can work with a design professional. It's why we're called "Interior Options."

A mix of eight patterns in a palette of yellow, marigold, blue, and white creates a cheerful but not busy scheme. No wall long enough to accept a queen bed necessitated the placement of the bed in the center of the room.

Designed for a man with eclectic tastes, a non-traditional color scheme complements the mix of traditional and modern furniture in this study/bedroom.

All references to the usual tile look have been removed in this bath by adopting a deeper version of the colors in the adjacent study/bedroom. A paneled screen hinged like a door has been utilized to shield the toilet area from view.

James R.
Irving,
ASID

James R. Irving
13901 Shaker Boulevard
Cleveland
OH 44120
216.283.1991

My great passion is designing beautiful rooms. As a colorist-decorator, it is most important to capture the essence and persona of the client. Color and room arrangement are utmost. And I enjoy doing every last-minute detail. My client list includes second and third generations of the same family.

Mauve pink walls and a lovely
English floral fabric, Carlotta,
offset a superb collection of rare
and important antiques and
give a sense of serenity.

A magnificent dining room set for dessert invites one to relax in soft pink tones. A regal frieze at the ceiling enhances the room.

A bejeweled daffodil-yellow and red room enhances a superb art and antique collection, making for a dramatic room day and night.

JADH
Interior
Design

Jeanne-Aelia Desparmet-Hart
19 Roosevelt Avenue
Larchmont
NY 10538
914.834.7442

Jeanne-Aelia Desparmet-Hart's taste for simple and understated interiors comes from her life in France. Her love for freely mixing eras, ethnic styles, and surprising materials comes from her international upbringing, and her extensive world travels. Her preference is for warm, muted tones, comfortable and sophisticated furniture, and an eclectic range of accessories. Humor, whimsy, and uniqueness are always kept a priority.

The entrance hall was left bare to downplay its small size. The stair risers were painted to look like a giant checkerboard with whimsical curlicues stenciled on each square; a large beaded orange serves as a focal point on the wide handrail.

Desk, standing lamp, and chair from the 1940s exude sophistication. The curtains and custom straw carpet are in brilliant, sunny shades. The bed and semi-circular ottomans were designed by Desparmet-Hart, and all the fabrics by Atelier Christine Lambert.

The French touches: French impressionist paintings and Eiffel Tower. The small semi-circular console by the fireplace and the lamp on the far right are by Desparmet-Hart.

Thomas Jayne Studio, Inc.

Thomas Jayne
136 East 57th Street, #1704
New York
NY 10022
212.838.9080

Thomas Jayne Studio offers expertise in every aspect of interior decoration, including architectural planning, selection of finishes and furnishings, and project administration. The studio respects all period of decoration, and often makes historic properties comfortable for modern use within the precepts of sound preservation practices. Mr. Jayne is trained in architecture and art history and has a master's degree in American architecture and decorative arts from the Winterthur Museum program.

The client, an auction expert, required a formal dining room that could double as a writing room. The chandelier conceals a canopy of halogen lamps that brighten the room. Along with this light fixture, the collection of uniformly framed eighteenth-century engravings forms the principle architecture and decoration of the room.

This New York apartment was designed to combine the clients' colonial antiques with modern pictures. The color scheme was orchestrated to favor terra-cotta.

This small room was designed to house books on architecture and the allied arts as well as a collection of rare Indian baskets. Many of the firm's clients have extensive collections and need suitable backgrounds.

Noel
Jeffrey
Inc.

Noel Jeffrey
215 East 58th Street
New York
NY 10022
212.935.7775

One of America's leading Interior Designers, Noel Jeffrey, is known for daring color, historical references, and an architectural eye for placing furnishings. "A room must feel comfortable; it must invite you in," he says. His eclectic breadth of styles extends from 18th century neoclassical to English Traditional, Mission, Art Deco, and Modern. Finding the perfect objects to complete a project is another Noel Jeffrey hallmark. This search for quintessential furnishings has led him to design pieces neoclassical in style, such as tables with inlaid woods and gilding, along with rolled armed and Regency sofas.

The living room and dining room were designed to showcase very simple yet important twentieth-century objects owned by the client. Therefore, the design of the furniture itself is minimal, which draws the focus to the objects. The large bronze urn is by Frank Lloyd Wright.

Architectural references were created in this bedroom sitting area by designing a cabinet to house an entertainment system. The bold details on this cabinet echo the detailing on many antique buildings. This three-dimensional object balances the simplicity of the paneled head-board shown below.

Across from the sitting area in the bedroom, strong architectural detailing was achieved by uphol-stering the wall behind the bed in large squares, with leather buttons at the cross-section of every square. The wall became the headboard, which then became part of the architecture.

Ken Jennings Design, Ltd.

Ken Jennings
304 West 75th Street
New York
NY 10023
212.496.1149

My design objective is to create a room that reflects the spirit and personality of the client, and also facilitates his or her lifestyle, customs, and daily habits. When I see a space for the first time, the space speaks to me, asking to be reconstructed, arranged, or decorated in a way that is unique to the people who live in it. I also consider the level of light, the size and proportions of the room, and the outside views. I strive for rooms both beautiful to see and comfortable to be in.

An unimpressive entryway to this Fifth Avenue penthouse was transformed by replacing a window and single terrace door with elegant French doors. Marble and granite floor and steps, also part of the redesign, complete the graceful entrance.

Two rooms were combined into one to create a loft-like living/working/dining/entertainment area that easily accommodates a three-person work staff during the day and parties of sixty at night. A cozy library/guest room adjoins the space, all of which is finished with fine antiques and flea market finds for a classical, elegant ambiance. The total space is less than 1,100 square feet (99 square meters), but is perceived as much larger. The area is further enhanced by three sets of French doors that replaced windows and give access to a narrow landscaped terrace that once functioned only as a decorative aspect of the building's exterior facade.

Kerry
Joyce
Associates,
Inc.

Kerry Joyce
115 North La Brea Avenue
Los Angeles
CA 90036
213.938.4442

A love for detail and fine materials characterize Kerry Joyce's interiors. Able to work in a broad range of styles, he creates satisfying interiors that reflect the personalities and lifestyles of his clients. "I love good design as well as comfort and I take it as a challenge to create an interior that will satisfy both," he says. He believes strongly in the integration of architecture and interior design, having an affinity for both. "I reject trend or fad. Creating a timeless, enduring interior is very important to me."

A serene natural garden surrounds

this inviting verandah.

Swedish chairs silhouette against a tranquil garden.

The convex mirror reflects the cream, white, and mahogany of this lovely living room.

Kiser-
Gutlon
Associates,
Inc.

Daniel Kiser
568 Broadway, Suite 802
New York
NY 10012
212.343.0288

While form, function, comfort, and budget are the overriding disciplines that govern our design jobs, it is fulfilling a client's fantasy that is most satisfying.

The drawing room of this New York apartment commands sweeping views of Central Park. The aubusson carpet, old world weavers tapestry chairs, and Austrian Biedermeier antiques enhance the golden wheat color palette—a favorite of the client.

The master bedroom is dominated by a period Napoleon III bed that anchors the high-ceilinged space. Floral patterned linen fabric, onyx chandelier, and Frette bed linens add romance.

The dining room is gracious with Edwardian detail: 11-foot (3.3-meter) ceilings, beveled glass doors, and original wall moldings. Classic English furnishing owned by the family is combined with a French savonnerie carpet, an Empire chandelier, and juxtaposed by a muscular 1930s painting.

Diane
Alpern
Kovacs
Interior
Design Inc.

Diane Alpern Kovacs, ASID
4 Main Street
Roslyn
NY 11576
516.625.0703

Since establishing our firm more than twenty-five years ago, we have gained recognition for our commitment to livable design. A home or work environment should be defined by the people who use it, not vice versa. Responsiveness to a client's taste is our first consideration. Although we handle a large range of commercial and residential projects, we are best known for our sophisticated country interiors. Clean lines, simplicity, and finely wrought details give each project a unique stamp.

Craftsman-style ceramic tiles

become a focal point in an

English country library.

A library wall, replete with
Dr. Seuss quote, rolling ladder,
and high-tech electronics.

Bright white cabinetry, brass
drawer pulls, and checkerboard
tiles keep things light and airy in
this diminutive 12 foot x 12 foot
(3.6 meter x 3.6 meter)
country kitchen.

Charles
Krewson,
Interior
Designer

Charles Fleming Krewson IV
128 E. 72nd Street
New York
NY 10021
212.396.9000

My goal is to create visually stimulating interiors that are both cozy and functional. The first priority is always to create a reassuring sense of scale and proportion that provides a serene framework for colors, textures, and objects that reflect and complement the personality of the client.

In the sitting room of a young collector, oak paneling and floorboards were bleached and buffed to conjure an ambient glow in an otherwise dark 1920s apartment.

A country house bedroom with pewter colored floors, Tiffany blue walls, and a collection of yard sale treasures creates a haven from city life.

A mantel in the Italian Renaissance style was installed with a pleasing array of objects spanning the twentieth century for the Georgian entry hall of a New York showhouse.

Michael R.
La Rocca
Ltd.

Michael R. La Rocca
150 East 58th Street, Suite 3510
New York
NY 10155
212.755.5558

The interior design signature of Michael La Rocca is recognized for gracefully honoring the architectural character, the location, and the particular needs of each client. Equally fluent in period, traditional, and contemporary design, a client initially defines a lifestyle and taste, and together enthusiastic strides are made in creating a beautiful yet functional environment. Experimenting with new ideas and communication are the vital keys in achieving a successful project.

A dining room that is both rich and spare incorporates a modern brass table base topped with Roman marble and antiqued Biedermeier side chairs covered in a black linen. The Italian mirror with gilded lion guards a stark directoire-inspired table designed by Michael LaRocca.

A master bedroom suite for a Southampton show house features a beautiful red paisley floral sleigh bed surrounded by a simple mixture of Venetian neoclassical furnishings, fabrics, and carpeting.

The custom cabinetry designed by Michael La Rocca for a living room/dining room of a New York townhouse has a true Biedermeier quality. The room has a character of a nineteenth-century interior and utilizes 1840s French furniture.

Barbara
Lazarus

Barbara Lazarus
10 Fones Alley
Providence
RI 02906
401.521.8910

To fulfill my client's dreams through comfort, a bit of fantasy, and communication is my ultimate desire. I do not believe in a "look," nor do I believe a home is ever completed. It is important to me that my client feels it is their home, not mine, and good design is alive and lasting.

A mixture of textures and color, and antiques and contemporary items combine to create a fantasy display.

An upstairs sitting room, part
of a guest suite, is designed for
maximum comfort. Walls are
covered in French toile fabric.
Amenities include a large TV,
current reading, and an
antique French writing table.

Faux painted details in the master
bedroom, featuring dark walls
and contrasting light floors.

Lemeau &
Llana/
Llamarté

Llana Arrott Wyman
521 West 26th Street, Third Floor
New York
NY 10001
212.239.6743

The design firm's aesthetic for quality and taste shows in these rooms—all in an apartment that seems like a real house, full of surprise and fantasy: the converted hallway kitchen comes decked in brilliant terra-cottas, sea greens and tiles of an ultramarine hue. This hallway leads to an informal eating area and a guest room with fabric on the walls and loads of exotic pillows. The formal living room, loaded with Victorian patterns on furniture and floor, features beautiful gilded and bronzed gates over glass doors that lead to a garden courtyard.

The Moroccan dining area—

for overnight guests and

long dinners.

The living room leads on to a walled exterior. The heavily colored Victorian functioned contrasted wonderfully augment golden yellow walls and gilded moldings.

Kitchen and passageway; The idea was to make this space so surprising, interesting and unusually busy that one would easily forget that it was functional as both.

Jeanne
Leonard
Interiors,
Inc.

Jeanne Leonard Going
10 Beach Road
Westhampton
NY 11978
516.288.7964

I enjoy the diversity of traditional and contemporary design, whether it be a residential or commercial project. I work closely with my clients to bring out their individual tastes and personalities, creating a warm, comfortable, and familiar surrounding to fit the way they live and work. My design goal is to have all of my projects remain valid with the passing of time.

The family room of this Long Island beach house was designed with natural straw tones on the walls and natural wicker furniture, giving it a soft, casual feeling. The vibrant fabric and colors in the area rug also add an inviting informality.

"Function first" was the theme for this grand kitchen, which contains every amenity as well as a warm space for dining.

Pillowed limestone walls, combined with granite floors and counter surfaces, invite the water views and sun into this room, creating a relaxed and romantic atmosphere.

Letelier and Rock Design, Inc.

Jorge Letelier and Sheryl Asklund Rock
1020 Madison Avenue
New York
NY 10021
212.988.2398

Our style is the result of our belief that good design is dependent on the relationship between architecture, space, geography, and the specific needs of the client. We favor calm, serene, and timeless design. Our work, averse to trends, is based on a strong knowledge of history, architecture, comfort, and an awareness of ever-changing technology.

Quiet reading corner with eighteenth-century Venetian red lacquer writing table and giltwood chair. Ashwood bookcases by Letelier & Rock. Nineteenth-century tole lamps and Pompeiian vessels grace a tabletop. Graphite on paper on walls is by Koenigstein.

Sofa, chairs, and coffee table are by Letelier & Rock. The wall features a silver birch silk panel, and a silver birch sisal covers the floor. Pompeiian vessels and a Roman marble bust are placed on end tables. Oil painting is by Pincment.

All furniture by Letelier & Rock is custom-made for this room. Linen scrims at the windows are also by Letelier & Rock. The room features ashwood and steel lamps, brushed steel sconces, ashwood sofas with zip-off cushions, and bookcases.

Tonin
MacCallum
ASID Inc.

Tonin MacCallum
21 East 90th Street
New York
NY 10128
212.831.8909

My work can best be described as eclectic; I pride myself on being an interpreter of my clients' dreams and needs rather than being a "signature" designer who creates only one recognizable style. The challenge is to create homes that reflect my clients' lifestyles and personalities. Working in different styles and periods for different clients is what excites my creativity.

The corner of a woman's bedroom in a townhouse done in light colors, contrasted with black lacquered antiques.

A bath in the same Victorian house, showing white architectural details against a ground of classic French wallpaper.

A view of a living room with red walls and white ground chintz to emphasize the whimsical architectural details of this Victorian house.

Robert
Madey,
AIA,
Architect

Robert Madey
1175 Montauk Highway
West Islip
NY 11795
516.587.4199

To create a home that has unique characteristics that represent a client's needs—whether the home is contemporary or traditional—the design should allow both work and play with the greatest ease and pleasure.

Private work/study room with traditional leather floors and a handpainted mural on the ceiling.

A view from a master bedroom
suite overlooking the waters
of Long Island Sound.

The view from the modern
kitchen looks through the indoor
pool area of this coastal home.

Brian J.
McCarthy,
Inc.

Brian McCarthy
1414 Avenue of the Americas
New York
NY 10019
212.308.7600

The ability to listen to one's client is the key to the success of any great project. Backgrounds form the foundation for any job, both architecturally and decoratively. The personality of a room is defined through the evolution of one's taste and curiosity. I encourage clients to develop their point of view through the decorating process. Their homes become a scrapbook of their lives and their passions. Romance, tranquility, and youth are three of the adjectives that best exemplify the rooms that I feel are most successful.

For a client insistent upon an office which reflected his strong personality and passion for quality and detail, this room began around a grid of mahogany paneling. The strength of Biedermeier and 1920s Art Deco furniture and paintings married well with the background.

In a room without architectural integrity, we combined simple early twentieth-century details, the clients' collection of Cubist paintings, and neoclassical furniture to create a layered and welcoming environment.

For young clients with a collection of very strong twentieth-century paintings, our objective was to achieve clarity of line and simplicity of form by using early nineteenth- and twentieth-century furniture with simple materials.

McMillen,
Inc.

Katherine McCallum
Bill Kopp
Sybil Calhoun
212.753.5600

Founded on the relationship between design and decoration, McMillen, Inc. believes that harmonious interior architecture is a prerequisite to the selection of furniture, fabric, and finishes. The firm particularly values gracious and welcoming rooms that reflect the personalities of their inhabitants. Comfortable seating, easy flow, and great lighting are important, whether the room is country cozy or city chic. Suitability, the firm also believes, requires consideration of the architecture and characteristics of the location as well as the needs, tastes, and preferences of the client.

A wonderful mix of subtle opulence enhances this dining room. An Italian Regence gilt console and a pair of George III giltwood torches (c. 1775) flank a six-panel Japanese paper screen (c. 1716). They complement a needlepoint rug (c. 1840) that once belonged to Mona Bismark.

Reflecting the client's love of flowers
and architecture, the palladian
windows surrounding this room
bring sunshine and life to the floral
chintz and needlepoint carpet.

Local stone was used for the
chimney in this Vermont living
room, where large, comfortable
sofas and chairs, mellow pine
furniture, and interesting folk art
contribute to the relaxed, country
look the owners enjoy.

Meadowbank
Designs Inc.

Penny Christie
Box 168
Bryn Mawr
PA 19010
610.525.4909

Each project is a chance to create magic, to turn an ordinary space into a delectable living experience. The challenge, creating an environment tailored to the needs and expectations of the client, means Meadowbank must view each project from a truly unique perspective as we weave our ideas together. We explore the options for elegant living and aesthetic pleasure for a truly personal environment.

The clients' love of the great American West was inspiration for a space that would showcase their spectacular art collection and provide them with the utmost comfort.

A cozy dining room brings together antique treasures and provides a dramatic setting for the riding portrait of a relative. The colors in the custom carpet further enhance this warm and intimate dining space.

Through the use of antique baskets, European wall tiles, and original barn beams, a commodious kitchen with the charm of a European country cottage was created for an active family.

Sandra
Morgan
Interiors,
Inc.

Sandra Morgan
31 Brookside Drive
Greenwich
CT 06830
203.629.8121

I agree with William Morris (1834–1896), the English writer who said "Have nothing in your houses that you do not know to be useful or believe to be beautiful." My goal is to achieve balance between function and aesthetics. A successful room must work well and feel good, in addition to looking beautiful. Comfort is primary, along with quality, attention to detail, appropriate lighting, and an inventive use of color. The partnership between my clients and myself is built on this foundation. Together we create a unique environment that enhances enjoyment of life.

Pencil-pleat detail at the top of the curtains in this airy breakfast room reinforces the graceful curve of this Palladian window. The green-and-white-checked chair seats and diamond-stenciled floor provide crisp graphics as a foil for the busy linen print. The overall effect is one of casual elegance.

The owner's love of grapes made this fruit-patterned fabric a natural choice for an informal seating area adjoining the kitchen and breakfast room. The tongue-and-groove paneled walls and ceiling add architectural excitement to this well-used space.

Granite countertops in an unusual sienna brown add character to fresh, white-paneled cabinets accented with brass hardware. The diamond pattern of the stenciled wood floors visually expands the space in the traffic areas surrounding the center island.

Nancy
Mullan
ASID,
CKD

Nancy Mullan
204 East 77 Street, #1E
New York
NY 10021
212.628.4629

My principal objective in designing a home is comfort—physical comfort, of course, but visual and emotional comfort as well. I achieve this by combining classical elements with creative space planning, and making it all serve the needs and dreams of the client. Years of experience enable me to understand my clients' requests—each receives the personal attention necessary to truly reflect his or her own personality. My trademark has become a serene, clean, and luminescent look; I pride myself on designing rooms that people are drawn to, and will want to stay in.

A high-powered woman begins and ends each day in this refuge, refreshing and soothing her body and spirit, surrounded by her treasures—the people and objects she cherishes for their inner value.

This small bedroom for a teenager had neither closet nor bookcases. The solution included a cozy bed alcove that provides both, along with a trundle for sleepover friends.

This apartment is a good example of the firm's serene, clean, and luminescent look. The owner's collection of antique plates hangs behind the dining table, which seats eight comfortably.

Sandra
Nunnerley
Inc.

Sandra Nunnerley
112 East 71st Street
New York
NY 10021
212.472.9341

As with all of my projects, I spent a great deal of time with my client getting an understanding of lifestyle, attitude, taste and needs. This particular client is a unique combination of casualness and glamour and I wanted the decor to reflect these personal characteristics. In this project, our mission was to create an environment that suits the active lifestyles of the 1990s while complementing the formality of the traditional architecture and setting.

Neoclassic in reference, the custom dining table has a top of figured mahogany with gilt detailing on the pedestals and feet. A collection of blanc de chine porcelain is indirectly lit within the display vitrine, which is lacquered the same cherry as the walls.

The designer used a personal
favorite, soft chintz in pastel
tones, in a master bedroom that
gets a lot of morning light. The
59th Street bridge provides instant
identification with Manhattan.

The guest room is furnished
primarily with family antiques.
Fabrics are a combination of
linen, cotton, and wool.

Parish-
Hadley
Associates,
Inc.

Albert Hadley
305 East 63rd Street
New York
NY 10021
212.888.7979

Albert Hadley is defined by his keen sense of architectural detail and proportion, his carefully edited decorative schemes, sustained sense of tradition, and an inexhaustible curiosity for the new. His goal is to help clients realize more than they thought possible within the framework of their own tastes.

A fluted, framed oval mirror hangs above a Chippendale mahogany hall table that features a late eighteenth-century French terra-cotta bust and an assortment of books and objects.

A view of the designer's office at night. The large iron table is a Parish-Hadley design; the top is a special black lacquered paper by artist Mark Sciarrillo.

The licorice color lacquered walls of this conference room are an assemblage for a collection of classical furniture and contemporary art, beyond which is a seating group in the reception room.

Pensis
Stolz
Inc.

Albert E. Pensis
200 Lexington Avenue
New York
NY 10016
212.686.1788

Pensis Stolz, based in Manhattan and on Long Island, is known for its high-end residential work in the New York, Connecticut, New Jersey, and Pennsylvania areas. The firm has also completed projects in Massachusetts, the Bahamas, and Florida, and is currently involved in a decorating job in Utah. Albert Pensis, principal of the firm, was corporate design director of Bloomingdale's prior to founding Pensis Stolz Inc. He attaches great importance to marrying decor to architecture, an approach immediately apparent in his interiors, characterized by a strong sense of space.

The brown, beige, and dusty pink aubusson rug forms the core of the room, and the upholstery fabrics were chosen to complement the rug. The red Queen Anne secretary adds height and a cheerful color accent.

An important aspect of the decorating was to place the client's collection of antiques throughout the house, in addition to selecting wall and window treatments, fabrics, rugs, and upholstery to complement them.

Although the architecture of the room and the client's art collection are contemporary, the client wanted a traditional living room environment. The furnishings are a blend of Georgian and Queen Anne styles.

Designs By
Florence
Perchuk,
Ltd.

Florence Perchuk
127 East 59th Street
New York
NY 10022
212.932.0441

For more than twenty-five years Florence Perchuk and her associates have specialized in space planning and designing high-end kitchens and bathrooms. Whether designing a magnificent estate or small apartment, their design philosophy is to remain true to the original architecture. When working with modern interiors, the firm successfully creates a minimalist look that can be embellished through the years. In doing restorations, Designs By Florence Perchuk, Ltd. tries to be true to the period it is working with or to the original concept of the space.

This turn-of-the-century castle stone residence in Westchester, New York was used as a showhouse. Because of time restrictions it was impossible to gut the kitchen, so the firm restored the space and included some additions.

144

The designer's goal in spaces like this is to bring nature into the room; the windows have been draped with dried leaves to define the view, while leaving the windows uncovered.

Florence Perchuk, CKD, created three zones in this 600-square-foot (54-square-meter) kitchen: working, sitting, and dining. For a touch of fun, walls and counters surrounding the hearth are adorned with Italian tiles painted with balloons.

Peter
Charles
Associates
Ltd.

Peter Charles Lopipero
17 East Main Street
Oyster Bay
NY 11771
516.624.9276

Peter Charles Lopipero brings more than twenty-five years of experience into residential and corporate design projects, with both period and contemporary interiors. He encourages client participation and interaction; the needs and purpose of a particular space create the impetus for the design project. The end result is an aesthetically pleasing and functional environment that reflects the lifestyle of those who inhabit its space.

An eclectic mix of English and Oriental accents and beautiful custom woven area carpets add up to sophisticated elegance.

This small 1950s kitchen was transformed into an elegant room and convenient workplace for the most discriminating of chefs.

This magnificent French country dining room appears at once gracious and elegant. The country French buffet, with its fascinating detailed carvings, offers ample storage and creates a beautiful service area. The elegant fabrics, mustard-toned wall coverings, and fine antique furnishings blend to create a feeling of inviting warmth, and are sophisticated enough to entertain the clients' most important guests.

PGG Interiors

Phyllis G. Goldberg, ASID
P.O. Box 14427
East Providence
RI 02914
401.331.7077

Interior design is a three-dimensional art, a form of sculpture. Empty space is void needing to be sculpted. I am a "space sculptor," approaching each project as if I'm creating a livable work of art, using furnishings and color as the medium. I create realities by helping to bring livable, elegant, and timeless design into the lives of my clients. My philosophy includes the three "R's"—recycle, refit, and restore. My designs are meant to accept change, to be seasoned to taste by a family heirloom, or spiced with the addition of something newly acquired.

Lively colors, contrasting patterns, and an interplay of textures make this family's living and entertaining space warm, welcoming, and visually exciting.

The rhythm of repeated shapes in polished surfaces of wood, marble, and glass gives the illusion of space in a narrow master bathroom. Soft, creamy rose-beige marble accented by deeper rose marble laid on the diagonal makes this room appear wider.

Different textural wall treatments bring shadow and sheen to this dining/bar area. An accent wall treated to appear like aged terra-cotta meets a soft beige textured wall with a polished limestone finish.

Thomas Pheasant, Inc.

Thomas Pheasant
1029 33rd Street, NW
Washington
DC 20007
202.337.6596

Thomas Pheasant, Inc. established in 1980, is an interior design firm involved in high-end residential and commercial work. Each project is addressed individually, always with an aim to create an aesthetically pleasing impression of suitability, quality, and comfort. Extraordinary attention is focused on architectural details, which define the character of a space and allow the selection of artwork, antiques, and collectibles to reflect the client's personality and set the spirit of the room.

This detail of the dining room shows how simple form and white create elegant silhouettes.

Darkly painted paneling was stripped to reveal the natural pine of this library. Classic upholstery is covered in a neutral linen to relax the room. Ottoman and game table were designed by Thomas Pheasant.

The dining table, mirrors, console tables, bust pedestal, and sconces are all designed by Thomas Pheasant.

Joan Polk
Interiors

Joan Polk, ASID
6722 Curran Street
McLean
VA 22101
703.442.8388

Our projects evolve from senses and interpretations of our clients' interests, feelings, and lifestyles. It is from listening to them that we can convey who they are and where they've been. I believe that accessories truly exemplify a client's individuality. Our motto: there are no problems, only creative solutions. Our trademark is attention to detail.

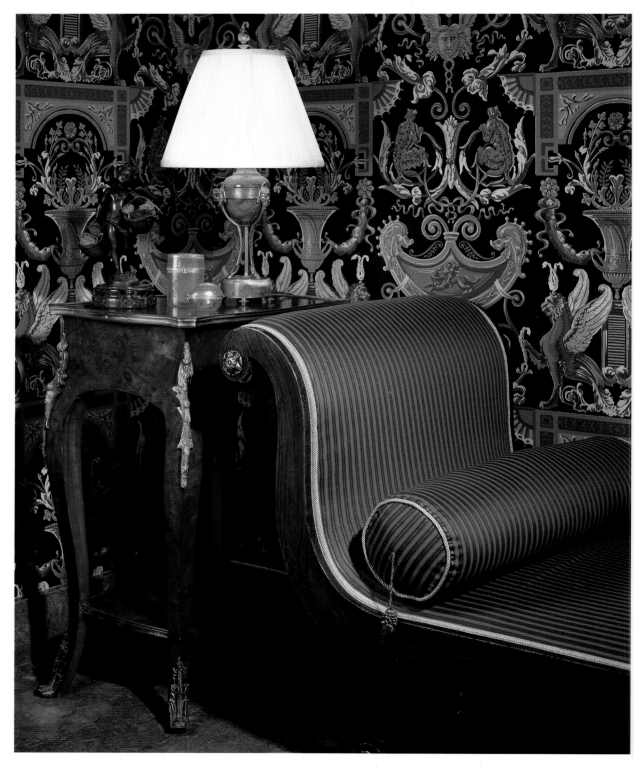

A dramatic backdrop sets an opulent tone for the antique furnishings in this ladies' repose.

The mingling of period pieces,
warmth and charm, and the use
of exciting fabrics and colors are
reminiscent of a time gone by.

Warmth, charm, and subtle
elegance are the hallmarks of
this inviting master bedroom.
Magnificent fabrics and out-
standing architectural details
complete the picture.

Josef
Pricci
Interiors

Josef Pricci
737 Park Avenue
New York
NY 10021
212.570.2140

The most important aspect of design and decoration is the relationship between designer and client. When the concept is jointly decided, the end result should be a very successful and memorable experience for both; and one that will continue in future projects.

This Southampton room was designed to seat twelve, with an additional table and wing back chairs for more cozy dining.

This is a very opulent room filled
with down furniture and antiques
created for ultimate luxury.

Gayle
Reynolds
Design

Gayle Reynolds, ASID, IIDA
7 Fessenden Way
Lexington
MA 02173
617.863.5169

My job is to inspire the client in new and imaginative ways while incorporating their personality, lifestyle, and preferences into a design. Their environments should meet their rational and emotional needs. As a result of my years of experience, I am able to offer my clients extensive resources, quality creative design, project coordination, and professionalism to the last detail. I want my clients to feel relaxed and secure while they work with me. Finally, I want them to have a unique sensory experience every time they enter a space we've created together.

Capturing the spirit of Cape Cod, this kitchen uses natural maple cabinets and feels very comfortable. The upper cabinet placement complements the varied lines of the ceiling.

Many of today's interiors reflect a small world of global travel. This ethnic living room has tailored Western upholstery, an antique bronze shutter from India transformed into a table, Mexican wood and leather chairs, abstract art, and a Tibetan rug. The feeling is natural and elegant.

A simple rustic Mexican cupboard holds special dishes and collectibles. This wonderful chunky wooden piece, surrounded by colorful art manuscripts, is seen from the entry area and sets the spirit of the house.

David
Ripp
Incorporated

David Ripp
215 West 84th Street
New York
NY 10024
212.362.7706

We create livable interiors that target the lifestyle of the client. We focus on the basics: clean, clear colors; classic furniture styles contrasted with contemporary upholstery and fabrics; respect for the surrounding architecture; a timeless blend without fads or trends. The design is comfortable, elegant, and approachable.

An adult, city apartment has soaring views of Central Park. The pale colors and selected antiques give a soft and stable background to daily life with tree-top views. Originally a two-story artist's studio, the balcony now serves as the master bedroom.

The design for this New York City dining room addresses the client's love for dramatic and vigorous entertaining. The wall and curtain colors originate in the antique tabriz carpet. The walls are glazed in a navy blue cross-hatched pattern and lacquered to a high gloss finish that reflects a candlelit room.

A classic modern house, built in 1960, restored to its original splendor with a new livability. The rug is an original design by Annie Albers, artist and wife of Josef Albers, the famous color theorist.

Lynn
Robinson
Interiors

Lynn Robinson
Powers Building
34 Audrey Avenue
Oyster Bay
NY 11771
516.921.4455

Be a good listener. Know the clients' lifestyle, favored colors, and style preferences. Create an environment that gives people pleasure. The style and proportion of an interior design should complement, balance, and harmonize with the house's own architectural integrity. I favor warmth and elegance, nothing to excess, but an emphasis on detail and performance. Good design is an investment for the homeowner. Rooms should have staying power that won't look dated in a few years.

A brick-enclosed staircase, Wilton carpet by Rosecore, and elegant documentary wallpaper from F. Schumacher combine for a look that agreeably spans the jump from rustic to elegant.

160

Wide antique floor boards with distressed charm, handmade Windsor chairs (available through Lynn Robinson Interiors) and an old hutch hand painted in a soft plaid by artist Julie Marten make this breakfast room cozy with a dressed-down sophistication.

Deep cherry walls with white moldings and a custom designed bookcase/dry bar make a bold statement softened by yellow florals, Persian rugs, and exquisite accessories. This room was designed to stand up to the test of time and eight grandchildren.

Pedro
Rodriguez,
F.A.S.I.D.

Pedro Rodriguez
2215 Locust Street
Philadelphia
PA 19103
215.561.3884

After immigrating to the United States, I studied at the New York School of Design. In the late 1960s I established my own design studio. I consider myself blessed to have had clients, many of whom have become personal friends. Providing them with beautiful surroundings that reflect their own taste, I was also able to fulfill their functional requirements. I hope that the future allows me the chance to continue in the profession that "chose me" so that I may continue to bring happiness and beauty to those seeking it.

In this late nineteenth-century home designed by Frank Furness, the ceiling and floor are original. The room is full of period objects, including the tabriz rug, the dining chairs, and the French cupboard.

The architecture is very old world, but this living room called for simple, clean-lined, contemporary furnishings. Color and pattern were kept to a minimum to accentuate the cheetah carpet and the exceptional collection of artwork and accessories.

Originally constructed as an outdoor porch, the room was enclosed to provide a family room. The copper-hooded fireplace does double duty by providing a focal point as well as additional warmth on cold evenings.

Dennis
Rolland,
Inc.

405 East 54th Street,
Suite #9-L
New York
NY 10022
212.644.0537

Dennis Rolland creates sumptuous and imaginative interiors for his clients that reflect their varied and cosmopolitan lives. He has a depth of knowledge in art and antiques, and an exigence for quality and detail in his furnishings, fabrics, and finishes. Dennis Rolland, Inc. was formed in 1987; prior to that he worked with Mark Hampton, George Clarkson, and at the John Wanamaker Interior Design Department in Philadelphia. He studied Interior Design at Michigan State University, and has lectured at New York University.

An eclectic mix of silks, velvets, linens, and taffetas enhances unusual furnishings and accessories throughout the salon. A theatrical Andre Dubreuil iron and glass torchère is set against a backdrop of a mirror and satin and taffeta curtains.

The owner of this Southampton, N.Y. farmhouse wanted to display a collection of Russian furnishings and accessories in a formal environment. The yellow and blue color scheme goes from the palest shade of yellow to brilliant blue in a sophisticated take on a tried-and-true color combination.

This dramatic salon for a famous New York modern art dealer was designed to complement a vibrant collection of art. The room incorporates a variety of unique and luxurious finishes created by a talented group of artisans, including a graphite ceiling and pigmented beeswax encaustic walls. The daring jewel-tone color scheme was inspired by the Stephen Mueller painting over the sofa.

Marilyn H.
Rose
Interiors,
Ltd.

Marilyn H. Rose
4 Birch Hill Road
Locust Valley
NY 11560
1.800.MHR.3003

My approach to design is a classical one. By using timeless color palettes, patterns, and design, I like to fill rooms with a quiet sophistication that enhances the client's lifestyle. As an interior decorator for the past twenty-five years, I have worked on projects with styles ranging from formal antique to country casual. Each project is a unique challenge that invites new ideas and opportunities. My role as a decorator is to interpret clients' needs by observing their tastes and lifestyles, to provide an atmosphere that exudes warmth and promises both comfort and elegance.

A French Aubusson rug of black and gold with accents of red creates the focal point in this formal dining room. Black wallpaper with gold urns creates a Neoclassical feeling. The gold fabrics of the window treatments and chairs add to the formality of the room.

The richly crafted green marble, softened by the designer wallpaper and custom draperies, adds to the elegance of the master bath's architectural detailing.

This room reflects English country elegance. Soft warm rose tones on the wall create a welcoming effect. The family collection of accents and accessories adds the personality of the lives of the people who live here.

Rita
St. Clair
Associates,
Inc.

Rita St. Clair
1009 N. Charles Street
Baltimore
MD 21201
410.752.1313

Interior design must not only be beautiful, but also responsive to the client's program, budget, and the public's acceptance. Rita St. Clair Associates has established an international reputation for beautiful, elegant interior design of contemporary and restored spaces. Utilizing color, form, texture, and light, the firm fabricates and subtly orchestrates many diverse elements to shape the client's environment and create enduring spaces. Working with commercially produced furnishings and custom one-of-a-kind elements allows the firm to realize budget constraints without compromising design.

The designer worked with Gauguin-like colors such as greens, purples, and marigolds to provide a sheltered environment for this glass and limestone pavilion-like space. Softly upholstered cushioning on a platform became the dividing space between the living room. The contemporary, oriental design creates casual elegance.

This living room evolved after a renovation of a newly empty nest household. The client wanted a comfortable room with abundant seating capacity. Bookcases were added for symmetry and to showcase the client's collectibles, art, and family photographs. Bright colors were used throughout.

In this Baltimore harborfront penthouse, Art Deco architectural drawings surround what is no longer a typical fireplace opening. A custom designed mantel includes two polychromed Indian elephant-shaped corbels and reinforces the design statement for the room.

Scott
Salvator,
Inc.

Scott Salvator
308 East 79th Street
New York
NY 10021
212.861.5355

Scott Salvator provides custom personal residential and commercial interiors dictated by the client's style, the architecture of the interior, and the location of the residence. His designs are eclectic, combining the best elements from various periods. He also stresses symmetry combined with comfortable elegance that flows from one room to another. Scott Salvator creates quality rooms that provide timeless visual pleasure through his use of antiques, upholstered furniture, color, and lighting.

The master bedroom at its most theatrical. The four poster bed is draped in a linen chinoiserie used throughout the monochromatic celadon room.

A wall of faux-antiqued mirror provides drama and space to an entry consisting of a formal composition of a pair of eighteenth-century sconces, a chinoiserie lacquered chest of drawers, Chippendale chairs, and a Venetian mirror.

A country library in an American pre-Revolutionary house has been treated in an eclectic manner. A traditional linen floral fabric and needlepoint rug have been combined with a mirrored wall and Chinese lacquered coffee table.

Justine
Sancho
Interior
Design, Ltd.

Justine Sancho
4827 Fairmont Avenue
Bethesda
MD 20814
301.718.8041

My firm is dedicated to customer satisfaction. Each client has an individual style—our goal is to work with clients to develop successful designs that reflect their tastes and personalities. We collect the thoughts and tastes of each client, stretch their imaginations, and then create a comfortable timeless interior. Close communication, patience, and attention to detail are trademarks of our firm. We work closely with clients to clarify objectives and set priorities. This collaboration helps clients avoid costly mistakes and stay focused on creating exciting interiors that enhance their lifestyle.

This master bedroom is a tranquil

cocoon that soothes and pampers

the senses in a setting of silk,

satins, and pearls.

Strong color and two seating areas anchor this narrow guest sitting room. Its low ceiling is camouflaged with a sheen-on-sheen diamond pattern, which adds height to the room.

The dining room is enhanced by silver leaf, a detail that creates a light, reflecting ambience suitable for both day and evening entertaining.

173

Cesar
Lucian
Scaff,
Inc.

Cesar Scaff
9 Nantucket Court
Beachwood
OH 44122
216.831.2033

This dining room demonstrates Schaff's design philosophy: With its exquisitely carved woodwork, it is part of a gracious stone house built in the first quarter of this century. In designing these areas we took full advantage of its possibilities—the dining room walls were left in their original faded paint, as was the breakfast room with its chinoiserie decoration. The furnishings could be no less important than the architectural surrounding; we chose antiques from various periods. The Knoll dining table adds counter point.

An eclectic mix of art surrounds the dining room fireplace, including a horse figurine from the Tang Dynasty, eighteenth-century Chinese porcelain plates, and sixteenth-century Italian polychrome candleholders. The painting to the right of the fireplace is by George Harlow, circa eighteenth century.

The breakfast room was transformed from a mundane space into a "ladies writing room." The enhanced space includes a desk in satin wood, painted in the manner of Angelica Kaufman, a Regence chair, and snuff boxes from the eighteenth century. The room retains its original chinoiserie decoration.

This splendid dining room with exquisitely carved woodwork is part of a gracious stone house built in the first quarter of this century. The dining room, which faces the loggia, features a seventeenth-century English chest and a painting by Allen Ramsey of the second Duke of Argyle.

Janet
Schirn
Design
Group

Janet Schirn
DC: 202.554.0017
Chicago: 312.222.0017
NY: 212-682-5844

Creativity, sophistication, comfort, classicism, timelessness, individuality...these character-ize our work. Architectural orientation, lighting, and art are important to it. Client person-ality, needs, objectives, and attitudes are reflected in each project, creating highly individual personal expressions. Excellent design, whether cutting-edge or traditional, is our goal, as is excellent service, whether individual or corporate.

Three small, gray offices are
restored to their original splendor
with strongly contrasting trim color,
which emphasizes the exquisite
original architectural detail in this
elegantly proportioned room.

The melding of contemporary upholstery and eighteenth-century antiques into a conservative, comfortable, social space speaks to the clients' dignity and refinement.

In a home used primarily at night and for entertaining, designer requisites were comfort, visual interest, display of diverse art objects, and the melding of old and new.

Teri
Seidman
Interiors

Teri Seidman
150 East 61 Street
New York
NY 10021
212.888.6551

Teri Seidman is the author of *Decorating Rich* and *Decorating for Comfort,* and her work has been featured on CNN "Style" and The Oprah Winfrey Show. Her philosophy: The process and product of interior design should be comfortable, beautiful, and full of joy.

Old World Elegance. Exuberant
tomato red and saffron yellow give
zest to this two-hundred-year-old
traditional home.

Scrubbed pine table atop hand-
painted "cobblestone" floor,
with greenery and iron, create
a garden mood and enhance
the country charm.

Deep club chairs swivel to fireplace or entertainment center,
surrounded by blue-glazed
walls punctuated by yellow. It all
adds up to opulent comfort.

Shields &
Company
Interiors

Gail Shields-Miller
43 East 78th Street
New York City
NY 10021
212.794.4455

Timeless interiors are inviting, intriguing, and softly polished. They should reflect the lives of the inhabitants, and should possess an admirable aesthetic standard. A delicate balance between the client, the interior designer, and design tradition can magically transform the ordinary into the special. When every detail blends together, an ambience is created that is unique, yet comfortable. Ultimately, the designer must be efficient, timely, practical, and extremely professional in order to satisfy the desires of good clientele.

Unusual turn-of-the-century architectural details and an elegantly draped window are counterpoints to luxurious sofas and club chairs in this urban great room.

Several shades of soft taupe and
rose make for an elegant mix of
color and furnishings in this country house living room.

This small but highly functional
kitchen can accommodate anywhere
from two to twelve for dinner.

Jean P.
Simmers,
Ltd.

Jean P. Simmers
24 Smith Street
Rye
NY 10580
914.967.8533

Good design is a composite of many things. It is the result of interpreting the clients' needs and feelings for their surroundings so the finished product is a seamless statement of their interests. It is quality in all areas of the work to be done. It is a home that is inviting, personal, and functional. At its best, good design appears to have evolved over time. My style: crisp traditional with use of antiques.

The husband's study is paneled in pine and painted a strong green color. The armless suede-covered sofa and chair allow seating not otherwise possible in this small room.

The master bedroom is done in ocean blues. Unlined silk curtains catch the summer breeze. An antique "friendship quilt" covers the foot of the New England four-poster bed, and a pair of Gould hummingbird prints serve as a reminder that the real ones are just outside.

True to the period of the house, the dining room is furnished with eighteenth- and nineteenth-century pieces. The eighteenth-century Dutch chandelier hangs above a Hepplewhite dining table. The nineteenth-century maple chairs are New York.

Siskin
Valls Inc.

Paul Siskin
21 W. 58th Street
New York
NY 10019
212.752.3790

Good design should be timeless. My work incorporates pieces from many different periods. The most interesting pieces are those that were designed a hundred years ago and yet could be mistaken for modern. The common element is usually simplicity. My work is bound together by this notion of simplicity.

All the clutter associated with a

psychiatrist's office is contained

neatly in the leather wrapped,

studded bookcase.

A chair awaits the mistress of
the house in an attic retreat,
perfect for moments of
self-contemplation.

The mistress of the house can sit in
her nineteenth-century settee and
gaze at the crystal ball.

Solutions By
Susan Ley
Dearborn,
Inc.

Susan Ley Dearborn
Palm Beach
561.835.8979
Boston
617.235.2920

Our philosophy: Good design is forever. Our strength lies in our ability to listen to our client's needs, to communicate throughout the duration of the project, and to pay close attention to budget and time projections. This threefold design philosophy saves our clients money, aggravation, and time. Practicality ensures clients a functional, personalized design statement suitable to their lifestyle. Service and support throughout the project from initial meeting to final installation means hours of saved time and freedom from frustration for the client.

Built as an addition to a stone castle high on the rocks overlooking the Atlantic, this room was designed as a woman's sitting area and card playing room.

This sitting room is a treasure chest of neoclassical French, English and American antiques and collectibles.

This charming custom cherry and marble kitchen/ family room adjoins a small galley kitchen.

Cindy
Stebbins/
Rinfret,
Ltd.

Cindy Stebbins
5 Lewis Street
Greenwich
CT 06830
203.622.0000

Cindy Stebbins/Rinfret, Ltd. strives to create interiors that are timeless, elegant, and appropriate.

A sophisticated and comfortable

media room.

Casual elegance defines a
Connecticut family room.

A girl's fantasy becomes
her real-life bedroom.

Stedila
Design
Inc.

Tim Button and John Stedila
135 E. 55th Street
New York
NY 10022
212.751.4281

Distinguished residential and retail projects typify Stedila Design Inc., which has a flair for interpreting a gamut of styles and periods in fresh new ways. Their work encompasses faithful, historically accurate restorations, originally designed contemporary or traditional environments, and sweeping transformations. The firm's commercial work includes high-tech showrooms, dynamic executive offices, and inviting retail spaces and restaurants. A sense of timeless style and a commitment to creating highly personalized spaces in which to live and work are the hallmarks of Stedila Design.

A man's retreat: high-tech computer hook-ups, touch pad control of lighting, audio/video, and window treatment, all accesible from the bed. Eat, sleep, and work without getting up.

A live-in kitchen in an 1890s ocean-front "cottage" had to be stripped down to the studs due to a previous design "makeover" in the 1970s—complete with harvest gold Formica counters and acoustical tile ceilings. The challenge: making the large state-of-the-art kitchen convenient for one chef or several —and in keeping with the period of the house

Carl
Steele
Associates,
Inc.

Carl Steele, ASID
1606 Pine Street
Philadelphia
PA 19103
215.546.5530

A room should be aesthetically pleasing and at the same time functional. The individual touches above and beyond the basics of furniture, fabrics, and color give the room its special character and make it complete.

A dining room in a Federal house features antique furniture, drawings by Robert Motherwell, and custom carpeting by Stark.

The clients of this pied-a-terre have an extensive contemporary art collection, including a three-dimensional painting by Arman, and bronze sculpture by Anthony Caro.

In this family sitting room, the painting over the sofa is by Elaine Kurtz and the drawing over the chair is by Picasso. All furniture is covered in Fortuny Ashanti design.

Stingray
Hornsby
Interiors

Ronald Mayne and DeBare Saunders
5 The Green
Watertown
CT 06795
860.274.2293

Our interiors reflect the aspirations and personalities of each client; no two jobs are alike. We use what we know of history, antiques, materials, proportion, color, texture, and light to create the appropriate interior, ranging from white-walled contemporary to drawing-room opulent. Meticulous craftsmanship and a jeweler's attention to finish and detail guide our work, even where there seems to be no detail. Continuity throughout a house is important; our interiors shun the trendy, aiming instead for a sense of timelessness, giving the impression that a room has always been there.

Antiques, accessories, lighting, carpet, wallpaper, and reproduction settee—all with an "exotic" oriental feeling—create layers of pattern on pattern, complementing every surface in this sitting room.

Historic restoration of a circa-1850 Victorian villa. Entrance foyer displays museum-quality nineteenth-century American furniture, art, and accessories, highlighted by custom-colored documentary patterned carpets and "heraldic" window treatment. A period stained glass window added on the street side of the house provides privacy and "sets a mood."

A stylish country cabin retreat evokes an eclectic "chic" style of the 1920s. The focal point is the old wood cathedral ceiling, balanced by off-white walls, and floor, furniture, and blinds in pale, neutral shades. The patterned faux leopard carpet, pillows, and red lacquer table provide a punch with pattern.

Karen
Sugarman
Interiors

Karen Sugarman
185 North Main Street
Andover
MA 01810
508.475.2930

The relationship between designer and client should be a partnership where ideas can be freely exchanged. The designer should pay careful attention not only to what the client is saying, but also to the subtle cues that emerge during their collaboration. The result of these exchanges should be a room with ambience and charm unique to each client's personality.

A crisp autumn afternoon, a sunny window, two shintoaster chairs and a pot of cocoa make a perfect setting for mother and daughter to catch up on the day's events.

A cheery monochromatic color scheme, coupled with the use of a glass table and a mirror floating between pilasters, disguise the diminutive dimensions of this model home dining room.

Once an enclosed porch, this master bedroom sitting room is transformed into an elegant music room. The brilliant sun is controlled by the use of rainbow hued silk panels combined with white silk Austrian shades.

Anne
Tarasoff
Interiors

Anne Tarasoff
25 Andover Road
Port Washington
NY 11050
516.944.8913

My approach to design is based on the integration of the client's lifestyle with emphasis always on comfort, patterns, and collections. I love to create romantic rooms that have an understated elegance, achieved with imaginative use of color and detail. I expect the end result to be a beautifully appointed, timeless room.

A romantic corner of a beauti-

fully appointed bedroom.

In this living room, sheer window treatments dramatically emphasize the crispness of the apple green walls.

A sybaritic bathroom designed for total indulgence.

Robert E.
Tartarini
Interiors

Robert E. Tartarini
516.338.0257
212.879.6145

Simplicity. A room should exude simplicity. My challenge is to design a room with functional and aesthetic purpose that also incorporates flexibility and individual expression. In order to make interiors harmonize with the living space, I must know my client well and seek timeless quality pieces that promote comfort and vitality.

The eighteenth-century portrait of Alfonso III d'Este by Leonardo Guzzardi welcomes guests to a traditional foyer.

The warm serenity of the blue and yellow color scheme enhances the drama of the Coromandel screen.

Blue and white Cowten & Tout fabric on the club chair plays to the timeless elegance of the red Chinese cabinet. The simplicity of the Irish crystal candlestick renders a peaceful tone.

Tolomeo
Ltd.
Design &
Decoration

Gerald C. Tolomeo
212.768.1660
973.742.8520

Gerald Tolomeo's penchant for mixing period and exotic furnishings along with contemporary designs enables him to create versatile rooms that project a look of serendipity. "To achieve the quality I strive for, my concept combines unexpected elements, within a single space. Together with sumptuous seating and a few items with a sense of humor, I feel elegance certainly can be attained without sacrificing comfort and ease."

In this guest bedroom, the

draped bed, makes for a quiet

and serene setting.

"The Conservatory" from the
Kips Bay show house in New
York City 1994.

A warm afternoon makes for a
perfect setting for "A hideaway"
in South Hampton, NY.

V-3 Design

Viorica Belcic
1212 Avenue of the
Americas, Suite 802
New York
NY 10036
212.222.2551

My goal is to carry out the wishes of my clients while tactfully guiding them towards choices of quality and taste, and at the same time being careful not to compromise professionalism.

The elegant dining and living areas pictured at right and on the preceding page were created with ornamental moldings made of a new fibrous cast plaster designed to look, architecturally, like an integral part of the ceilings and walls. Special lighting behind the draperies in the dining area adds a soft and romantic glow to the room.

A free-standing mahogany staircase marks this townhouse entrance hallway. Local craftsmen created the exquisite ironwork balustrade. The challenge presented by the large marble slab floor was successfully met by tailoring the pattern to the space and ensuring an exact fit.

Jean
Valente
Inc.
Interiors

Jean Valente, ASID
175 E. 79th Street
New York
NY 10021
212.472.4574

A home is an extension of one's self; a mirror of one's dreams and personality, and a safe place. Through innovation, individualism, simplicity of use, and elegant design, the decorator takes vision to substance.

The entrance hall floor was stripped to natural and stained with stencil border and starburst center motif as a contrast to the darker floors of the adjoining rooms. The gold-finished vaulted ceiling echoes the glow of striped wall covering.

The client's preference for contemporary art is a relief from the customary classical notes. The living room features a camel painting by Ben Schonzeit over the sofa, and a painting of a woman by Phyllis Diller over the period empire cabinet that serves as an open bar. Silk taffeta curtains and a print wall covering in vanilla give a glow to a formerly dark room; bamboo shades and sisal rug add a less serious touch.

Van Hattum & Simmons, Inc.

Peter Van Hattum and
Harold Simmons
225 East 60th Street
New York
NY 10022
212.593.5744

When Harold Simmons, a principal designer at Parish-Hadley Associates, joined the established firm of Peter van Hattum Interiors, a successful partnership was formed. They handle projects of such varied style and location as residences in London, Washington, New York and the Hamptons, embassies in South America, estancias in Argentina and a ski lodge in Vail, Colorado. Their use of antiques, combined with contemporary furnishings and a palette of diverse colors, textures, and patterns, gives a feeling of warmth and comfort to every room, no matter how formal or rustic that space might be.

This deep green lacquered living room was created in a Manhattan apartment for a couple with residences in several countries. The eclectic furnishings include an eighteenth-century Italian black lacquer writing table and a number of period French chairs.

The curtains, bed, and canopy in this master bedroom feature traditional English chintz trimmed with linen fringe against a soft blue striped wallpaper. An antique hand-painted folding screen with trompe l'oeil exotic birds rounds out a corner of the room.

The subtle colors of the upholstery and the rug, juxtaposed with dark glazed walls and various gilt and porcelain objects, create a dramatic background for evening entertaining.

Wagner
Van Dam
Design &
Decoration

Ronald Wagner and
Timothy Van Dam
853 Broadway
New York
NY 10003
212.674.3070

Our rooms are a celebration of life and of the people who use them. Each room reflects our client's individual personality, put forth with style and panache. We strive to create a balance in our interiors; comfort and sophistication are the two key elements that should harmonize in every notable room. Our success can be measured by our clients who return to us again and again because we offer them interiors in which to live and to live up to.

Shimmering damask wallpaper heightens the play of light and the rich level of detail in this sumptuous dining room.

The use of saturated color and zebra upholstery create a sense of mystery in this historic bedroom.

Built-in bookcases that complement the existing period mantle and exposed rafters give this townhouse living room an intimate character.

Walker
Design
Group

Lisa Walker
P.O. Box 80526
Phoenix
AZ 85060
602.952.2908

Arizona designer Lisa Walker does not believe in creating a signature look but allows the space to reflect the style, personality, and needs of the occupants. Her work is timeless, staying away from trends by choosing classic pieces and strong proportions that will look good in twenty years.

Responding to the client's taste—which favored a neutral, "timeless" palette—the designer used clean-lined, classic upholstered pieces with a mix of oriental fabrics and ethnic accessories.

The bedroom was designed for the ASID Phoenix Showcase house. The setting was a newly constructed "sixteenth-century French chateau" with a view overlooking a pond.

The canopied bed was tailored in white cotton matelassè, with natural linen bedcovers and dust skirt. The rough hewn plank flooring is set against a natural sisal rug, juxtaposing the rough material against fragile white cottons.

Elizabeth
Read
Weber,
ASID

Elizabeth Read Weber
79 East Putnam Avenue
Greenwich
CT 06830
203.869.5659

While her attitude on life might be described as playful, Elizabeth Read Weber, ASID, a third generation interior designer with more than fifteen years of experience, takes her business very seriously. Elements of her youthful approach, reflected in her current work, are color and whimsy. Color arouses the senses and changes the entire look of a space. Whether the highest level of chromatic value of a hue is shown in an accent pillow or expressed more dramatically on walls, ceilings or floors, color will always produce a different reaction—hopefully a pleasant one.

Hand-painted seafoam-blue stripes add a touch of whimsy to a formal entry foyer. The designer's favorite antique pink luster adds color to a demilune console.

Vibrant cool blue walls pronounce the red antique painted furniture and add depth to the room. Crisp blue and white fabrics from Cowtan & Tout and accents of red maintain the integrity of the atmosphere.

A very small living room in a carriage house presented the challenge of making use of existing furniture. A periwinkle-blue ceiling and linen-colored walls create a palette that easily blends with all colors.

David
Webster &
Associates

David Webster
254 West 25th Street
New York
NY 10001
212.924.8932

The designer's aim is to produce a coordinated and organized interior or exterior space that, at first view, looks neither consciously coordinated nor carefully organized. Styles he delves into vary from Adirondack lodge to Provincial farm house, but all the work reflects the wishes of the client. Architecture serves as the framework upon which decoration is hung; everything is orchestrated to produce interiors that are designed, but feel real.

The feeling of the ski house is more European than southwestern; the large Louis XIV armoire makes a very strong statement in the big living room.

In the Dining room, ebonized
Hoffman chairs with Green
Mohair seats and their
companion table (Commis-
sioned by ICF) produce an
understated yet decidedly
art deco feeling.

A 1920's Chinese carpet and
antique Architectural prints add
interest to the Art Deco inspired
Livingroom.

Weixler,
Peterson
& Luzi

2031 Locust Street
Philadelphia
PA 19103
215.854.0391

With backgrounds in architecture, design, and the decorative arts, Weixler, Peterson & Luzi was established in 1981 to address the needs of prestigious clients who seek a highly personalized attention to detail. The firm's work covers a broad stylistic range and has earned several design awards and wide publication. Weixler, Peterson & Luzi insist that "the role of a good decorator is to vanish." The firm frequently is selected by clients who want the design of their homes to reflect their lives and their interests.

This 11-foot (3-meter) square intimate sitting room is part of an extensive renovation to a townhouse that also included a luxury master bathroom, enlarged closet space, and an elevator.

The master bedroom in a Federal townhouse was redesigned from three smaller rooms. "The Offering to Bacchus," a Brussels tapestry woven in 1710, is from Chevalier and balances three high windows. The custom bed is upholstered in a Brunschwig & Fils texture.

In the master bathroom, antique Wedgewood Basaltes urns from Bardith sit in the windowsills, softened by Roman shades of a Brunschwig & Fils casement.

Sue Wenk
Interior
Design Inc.

Sue Wenk
300 East 71st Street
New York
NY 10021
212.879.5149

In creating an environment for the interior of a home, my approach is one that first focuses on the client rather than the actual space. I must listen to their needs in order to achieve a comfortable and functional living space. Working together with the client, we combine various colors, shapes, and textures to create a space that is both functional and comfortable. A successful design project will evolve over time into a space that best suits the clients and their lifestyle.

Brick wallpaper and an "awning" above the window combine with bright colored florals, ivy, and butterflies to bring the outdoors inside this dining room.

Rich colored walls and furnishings combined with the strong natural light provide a cozy haven for reading, watching television, or enjoying the company of friends and relatives.

A hideaway for young boys or a future astronomer comprises stars, suns, and moons on the walls and windows. The sturdy bunk beds and desk are both fun and functional and add to the element of nature.

Bunny
Williams,
Inc.

Bunny Williams
306 East 61st Street, 5th Floor
New York
NY 10021
212.207.4040

What really makes a great room is a combination of design and function that clearly represents the owners' tastes and lifestyle. One must always start with the "bare bones"—the architecture—and then move on to the colors and furnishings to create rooms that fit the inhabitants. My style is based on tradition, but with an eye on the future.

The interior of a New York living room showcases an eclectic mix of French and Russian furniture and contemporary art.

The dining room of a house in
Connecticut features a painted wall
canvas of garden scenes and
French chairs in original needle-
work around an eighteenth-century
English dining table.

A nineteenth-century French desk
graces an alcove in a living room in
Pennsylvania; an Italian landscape
painting hangs above a French
directoire console table.

Margot
Wilson
Interiors,
Inc.

Margot Wilson
4305 Westover Place, NW
Washington
DC 20016
202.244.2171

Quality is foremost. Use the finest objects, whether choosing art, furniture, or carpets. Then comes spatial clarity: analyze the space you are given to design, and select only the most meaningful and appropriate ideas. Workmanship: without excellence, no design will withstand the wear and tear of human beings or their animal friends. Attention to detail: subject each item in a room to ruthless scrutiny. The result of these criteria should be a certain synergy and serendipity, and classic timelessness appropriate to the space.

A 1927 Tuscany villa was the Washington DC National Symphony Decorators' show house for 1996. Soaring Gothic ceilings set off the long beige marble hall. Heavy stucco walls are faux finished in creams, pinks, and mauves.

Architecture dictated the decor; furnishings were serious, few, and large scale. A bronze whippet and a bronze rooster add humor to the Old World ambiance of this great hall.

Silvery green damask, gold and red Venetian striped silk, dark walnut woods, and black wrought iron sconces are set off by lunettes of Tuscany scenes painted above the antique Venetian doors. Bamboo palms in mahogany stands are used as accents.

John Robert Wiltgen Design Inc.

John Robert Wiltgen
70 West Hubbard, Suite 205
Chicago
IL 60610
312.744.1151

John Robert Wiltgen, IIDA, believes that the integration of art, architecture, and design is what makes his homes timeless.

The marble-clad fireplace, the focal point of the seating area in this long and narrow loft space, was created to contrast with the coarser textures of the brick walls and timber beams and ceiling.

In this Toronto loft, the hand-painted mural (on canvas) was specifically created to be wall-papered to the curved wall separating the bedroom space from the living and dining area.

The mosaics for the ceiling and tub of this bath look as if they were centuries old. Framed by slabs of Bottacino, each piece of marble, less than 3/4 inch (2 cm) square, was hand cut to avoid the effect of a perfect grid.

Miriam
Wohlberg
Interiors

Miriam Wohlberg
2325 Lindenmere Drive
Merrick
NY 11566
516.868.5066

We believe successful interior design reflects the taste and personality of our client. We continually look with joy at the many varied paths to achieving beauty and harmony, combining comfort, elegance and personal expression with a luxurious environment that will stand the test of time.

Silk cotton and voile draperies create an asymmetrical backdrop for a copper leafed chaise, creating a contemporary yet classic and romantic mood.

An arts-and-crafts style kitchen, reinvented for the '90s. Cherry wood cabinets, copper inserts and a red slate sink surround a hand-painted sand-blasted back splash recalling designs of Frank Lloyd Wright.

A view to fine dining in the smaller spaces of today. French iron gates, an antique cherry wood table and chairs of iron and tooled leather rest on a laser cut, herringbone floor in modern vinyl.

Vicente
Wolf
Associates

Vicente Wolf
333 West 39th Street, 10th Floor
New York
NY 10018
212.465.0590

With twenty-five years of experience I have gone through the range: from very minimal design to realizing that an environment requires many points of view. To have an
individual style, the only need is the point of views that are cohesive.

A breakfast room that doubles as a
sitting room is separated from the
kitchen by a low wall that hides a
stove on the other side. Open
shelves in the kitchen allow for
easy access to the china.

An eclectic mix of periods and ideas that range from a drop-leaf table found at a yard sale to a hand-woven linen rug creates a comfortable and inviting living room.

A Boisserie mirror, a Jean-Michel Frank table with pull-out leaf, a 1950s Boomerang table, and a modern upholstered bed give a master bedroom timeless quality.

Mark Zeff Consulting Group Inc.

Mark Zeff
260 W. 72nd Street, Suite 12B
New York
NY 10023
212.580.7090

I believe that comfort does not have to be compromised in the quest for the most aesthetically pleasing design. My love of natural fibers and natural materials is part of what the client expects and what I pursue. If you meld these basics with a truly tailored design and my passion for eclectic antique pieces, you will understand that function, comfort, and beauty can live together.

Africa meets Asia in the dining room. Antique Chinese chairs surround a Mark Zeff–designed table in hot rolled steel and white birch. The setting is complemented by a matching Mark Zeff chandelier.

The client wanted a haven from his hectic Manhattan life. The living room provides just that—tranquillity, simplicity, and a combination of old- and new-world charm with strategically placed antiques, and furniture designed by Mark Zeff.

The client requested something casual but elegant in this Sagaponack, New York, home. This Anglo-Raj influenced Anguilla bed comes from the designer's Afro-Caribbean-inspired collection.

INDEX OF INTERIOR DESIGNERS

INDEX OF PHOTOGRAPHERS

ACKNOWLEDGMENTS

The editors at Rockport would like to give special thanks to the following people who helped make this the best book it could be:

To **John Aves,** for his vision and constant quality-control checks;

To **Bill Rothschild,** who brought many new interior designers into the fold and whose photographs show the designers' work in the best possible light;

To **Dennis Krukowski,** who, like Bill, found many designers for the book and diligently followed up with excellent photographs;

To **Teri Seidman,** whose coherent introduction will help clients and designers communicate more clearly;

To **Billy Francis,** for his invaluable help in the early stages of this project;

To **Sara Day,** our tireless layout and composition artist who kept her cool through endless rounds of corrections;

To **Cindy Schimanski,** an editorial freelancer who helped on all stages of the book from the beginning up to the final checks; and

To **Todd Crane** in the Rockport sales department, whose efforts were invaluable in making this book come together.

BUTLER PUBLIC LIBRARY
BUTLER, PENNSYLVANIA 16001

747 SHO

Showcase of interior design.
Eastern, third edition.

747 SHO

Showcase of interior design.
Eastern, third edition.